The Wind in My Hair

The Wind in My Hair

by *Salwa Salem*
with *Laura Maritano*

translated by *Yvonne Freccero*

Interlink Books

An imprint of Interlink Publishing Group, Inc.
Northampton, Massachusetts

First published in 2007 by

INTERLINK BOOKS
An imprint of Interlink Publishing Group, Inc.
46 Crosby Street, Northampton, Massachusetts 01060
www.interlinkbooks.com

Text copyright © Giunti Editore S.P.A., Firenze-Milano, 2007
Translation copyright © Yvonne Freccero, 2007

Library of Congress Cataloging-in-Publication Data

Salem, Salwa, 1940–1992.
[Con il vento nei capelli. English]
The wind in my hair / by Salwa Salem ; translated by Yvonne Freccero.
p. cm.
ISBN-13: 978-1-56656-663-6 (pbk.)
ISBN-10: 1-56656-663-0 (pbk.)
1. Salem, Salwa, 1940–1992. 2. Women, Palestinian Arab—Biography.
3. Immigrants—Italy—Biography. I. Title.
HQ1728.5.Z75S2513 2006
305.48'89274045086914—dc22
2006014172

Printed in Canada

To request our complete 40-page full-color catalog,
please call us toll free at **1-800-238-LINK,** visit our
website at **www.interlinkbooks.com**, or write to
Interlink Publishing
46 Crosby Street, Northampton, MA 01060
e-mail: sales@interlinkbooks.com

CONTENTS

Introduction: Death and Memory

Houston, December 1990

Here I am in a hospital bed. Five days ago I was operated on for a lung tumor, and have since spent four days in intensive care. They have just given me something to ease the pain; I feel drugged. I am trying to find myself in this room where there is a television, a computer, a bathroom, a daily change of towels and soap, everything necessary and unnecessary, and a total silence that drives me crazy.

Yet I have been fortunate in my tragedy, treated by the best specialists, operated on by the best surgeon in the best cancer center in the world. I try to look on the positive side, at what has gone well. I cling to life as I always have.

But I am overwhelmed by the severity of the surgery, by the pain and above all by the weight of my loneliness. I have always tried not to be passive, but now there seems to be nothing more I can do. The disease is conquering my body, my soul, my willpower, my courage. I've told the doctors that I am still willing to struggle, to hope and to bear it with courage, to fight back so that I can have the privilege of continuing in this world and being a part of life.

I do not know why I love this life. Despite the difficulties I have always loved waking up each day; morning is the most beautiful moment. To get up at first light, sit in the kitchen over coffee, a newspaper, and a cigarette gives me the thrill of a new beginning every time.

I have always loved the changing seasons: the symphony of colors and the strong autumn winds, the white of winter with its cold that stops me in my tracks and makes me feel alive, the intense, bright green of spring, roses beginning to open up, the sounds and silence of summer. Changing and adapting to the nature of each season has been a constant pleasure.

Even though I have had to confront so many challenges, and even though the world around me is certainly not beautiful, I have always felt that it is our responsibility to try to change what is not working and to get pleasure from the little results that make us feel big and important. I want to go on participating, to make a contribution, to work, to see a free Palestine, to watch my children grow, to continue to protect them and give them love. I want to be with my friends and with many other wonderful people who have given me so much.

I hate the void, I hate disappearing, I hate feeling that I do not exist. I have always been very curious and the idea of vanishing, of being annulled, of not knowing any more about this world, of not having news of my friends, of the people I love—all this grieves me.

But no one is indispensable. Everyone is forgotten and I am just anyone. This is why I want to tell my story and make it into a book. It is something that my children and my friends will one day show to their children, and they will say: "We knew that person, we lived with her." And I will once again be alive among them, and among the others. It is important to me that people learn about my life; I do not want to go away without leaving my mark.

I close my eyes and think about my life, about the path I took before I came here, about my roots. I see again the lights of my homeland, the silver reflections of the fields of olive trees. I can smell the scent of orange blossom, the freshness of the air and the sun finally piercing through the first days of spring.

ONE

Palestine
1930s–1948

Beloved Roots

I can still see among the olive and citrus groves and the sparse hills, in the clear air of spring, Kafr Zibad, the village where my father was born. It is near the city of Tulkarem and not far from the sea at Jaffa, which is glimpsed from the hilltops in the distance.

During the 1930s—when my father was a boy—there were about 500 people living in Kafr Zibad. Kamel, my father, was the youngest of eight sons in a well-to-do farming family. They lived in a large house with many rooms facing onto a fine courtyard. That courtyard was the stage for the life of the women of the family, the scene of so many conversations, communal work, and problems shared among the women of the village.

Kamel was an alert boy, full of imagination, with an adventurous spirit. His mother Umm Jamal thought he had a dangerous character, so they began looking for a wife for him, thinking that it would help him to mature.

One day Umm Jamal went to the nearby village of Siffarin for a wedding feast. It was a typical rural feast in which the whole village participated: people came out in the streets, wandered the alleys, and visited the bride's and bridegroom's houses. The women intoned their *zagharit*, their greetings of good fortune. Everyone danced and sang and made music. The bridal couple arrived on horseback.

In the midst of all this confusion, Kamel's mother took note of Husniya, a lovely young girl of thirteen. Husniya was tall and wore the traditional gown, black with red embroidery on her chest and around the skirt. Two long tresses escaped from the scarf knotted around her neck. All the young girls danced with the natural ability of those who learned the agile undulation of their hips in childhood, but she, being so tall, moved with particular elegance. Every now and then she would stop and begin to play: her long fingers beat the rhythm energetically on her *tabla*. When she smiled her glance was lively and focused.

Umm Jamal was enchanted. She made up her mind: this girl would be her daughter-in-law, her Kamel's wife. The more she watched her, the more she was convinced that she was just right for Kamel, an energetic, exuberant girl. My grandmother continued to think about Husniya even after the feast. It is not easy to choose a wife for the son one loves. She chatted with other women and learned more about Husniya, as she took tea with them between her errands.

A month later she decided to return to Siffarin to ask for her hand. She took the important members of her family with her and was received by Husniya's parents. When Husniya brought the coffee into the room my grandmother began to speak about the bridegroom. She described him as a fine young man, tall, blonde, with big green eyes. She portrayed him as vivacious, lively, and resourceful. Then she talked about his one great mystery:

"Kamel owns a large trunk which he always keeps closed and no one knows what is in it... he says it is full of dreams and treasures." Husniya was struck by Umm Jamal's story. That mysterious trunk, that world of fantasy fascinated the young thirteen-year old girl who began to dream about the young man she had never seen. And so it was that, some time later, the two unknowns married each other.

Husniya left Siffarin and went to live in her husband's village. At Kafr Zibad everyone was fascinated by the new presence in their midst. They watched her when she left the house, walking proudly, her head always held high, looking straight ahead of her, determined to avoid the men's glances. When she went to the fountain she balanced the jar full of water on her head without holding it with her hands. All the men envied Kamel.

Husniya had not yet menstruated so she was not yet a woman. It was a fairly difficult situation but normal in those days. The husband was expected to wait for his wife's maturity, to make a fuss of her and treat her tenderly. I believe my father behaved this way because my mother has always been in love with him.

The British had occupied Palestine since 1917, and soon the Palestinian struggle against the occupier separated this very young couple. Kamel joined the partisans, was arrested in 1936, and condemned to death with ten of his companions. The death penalty was dispensed regularly, and sometimes with very little provocation, such as the possession of a knife. The British took partisans by night in secret to Wadi al-Badan, on the road between the mountains that stretch from Nablus to the Jordan valley. Outside the village, on the edge of a deep overhang, prisoners were regularly blindfolded, shot in the back, and their bodies thrown into the gulley, onto the gravel bed of the wadi, a small green stream. Wadi al-Badan remained a shady village with a cascade of pure water, a holiday destination for the people of Nablus. My people have never forgotten, but, like many other places in occupied Palestine, there is not even a stone there to remember the dead.

Years later, on those winter afternoons spent among relatives and family friends, I would often hear talk of the time of the British and of my people's struggle. The British governed Palestine with an iron fist: there was a military governor and the laws were cruel. What is more, there was an idea in the air of creating a "national homeland" for the Jews in our land. Jewish immigration had already begun at the start of the century, but it was an immigration of individual people or small groups. The Palestinians had welcomed them and had never had any problems with them, just as they had never had problems with the Jews who had always lived in Palestine. Things changed when they began to arrive in droves on British ships. It was then that the Palestinians of my father's generation understood that these people were coming to steal the place, that there was a plot and that the situation was getting dangerous. When the plan to build a Jewish state in Palestine became clear, the Palestinian people became inflamed.

The main Palestinian authorities had requested the constitution of a local government in which each of the three religions would be represented: Christians, Muslims, and Jews. The British rejected the proposal because it was counter to the promises they had made to international Zionism on behalf of Her Britannic Majesty. In 1936 strikes were called for and carried out by the Palestinian people en masse. The number of partisans grew by the thousands.

They were village men, ordinary people, who organized the resistance. Proud men, hurt by the behavior of the British, but not led by modern ideologies. It was a spontaneous struggle: the partisans had few weapons and no international support. Many were living in hiding, concealed in the mountains.

The figure of the messenger in family stories always fascinated me. The messengers were those who carried news from one group of partisans to the other, from village to village. I was struck by their knowledge of the Palestinian land, every centimeter and every tree—when it had been planted, how old it was, and to whom it belonged. Olives in our world are not merely trees: almost every one of our olive trees has a name, bound up in the story of the families, the people, the things and the places. I was fascinated by the messengers' devotion to the land, their crazy love for Palestine.

Kamel was still in prison after several months under arrest. His companions had been assassinated at Wadi al-Badan a few at a time, and he expected the same fate. Husniya stayed alone with Adnan, her first son, who had been born a few months earlier and was now her only companion. She was an energetic woman, full of dreams, a chatterbox, ironic, with a great gift for making up songs and telling fables. That was how she raised her son, always playing with him, telling him the history of the Arabs, narrating fairy tales and religious episodes, telling him about family events. Adnan grew into an active young boy with a lively mind.

Husniya owned a Singer sewing machine, quite a treasure in those times. She spent a lot of time sewing clothes for the partisans. She took part in the resistance, even hiding partisans in the well in the courtyard during searches and acting as the courier between the partisans hidden in the mountains and those in the village. She took risks, but it made her feel close to her husband who was condemned to death; it was her revenge.

The sewing machine was a present from Kamel's oldest brother who was taking care of her. A tall man, heavy-set and very elegant. His name carried a lot of weight in Kafr Zibad and in the surrounding villages. He, too, was a member of the resistance. He was known for his generosity and for helping people in need. During the catastrophe of 1948, when people were in need of everything, I remember him coming to Nablus and distributing food and provisions.

Months passed. The Palestinian revolt raged on and Kamel was still in prison waiting to be executed. Then, an unexpected miracle: the British, in an attempt to placate the rebels, granted an amnesty. After seven of his companions had been killed, Kamel was freed.

The experience of prison, of being condemned to death, and of his unexpected liberation marked him deeply. He aged suddenly, matured, became more attached to his family, more aware of what a precious gift life was; he began a new existence. The village of Kafr Zibad was too limiting. He no longer wanted to work in the country. He had big, new plans. So, shortly afterward, he moved with his family to Jaffa.

In Jaffa he started a successful wholesale fruit and vegetable business. He prospered to the point of being able to make loans to farmers to help them maintain their lands; in exchange, the farmers guaranteed him exclusive rights to their seasonal produce. He worked hard and had many employees. And, when he was not working, he read—big, ancient books on Arab history, such as Ibn Khaldun's, books of ancient travellers, our traditional poets, the Qur'an. The sophisticated language did not deter him, though he had only finished third grade in school. He had notebooks in which he gathered sayings, proverbs, and poems, and he wrote marvelous letters.

My mother had a womb that was programmed like a computer; she gave birth to a child almost every two years. My parents did not use any means of contraception, partly because of a lack of knowledge and partly because it was contrary to their beliefs. In order not to get pregnant, my mother breastfed the children, and when she stopped breastfeeding, another child would come along immediately. She always went to Kafr Zibad to give birth, because her mother-in-law was there and she could count on receiving all the help she needed. There, they would celebrate the rituals demanded by tradition. Issam followed Adnan, then in September 1940 I was born, and after me Ihsan, and then my sister Feryal in 1946.

Adnan and Ihsan were very beautiful babies, blond and blue-eyed; no one believed that the youngest was a boy, his features were so delicate. I was different—I had black hair and dark eyes, like my other brother Issam. Feryal, on the other hand, had brown hair and green eyes.

I have a truly golden memory of Jaffa and our wonderful prosperity. My older brothers went to school while I went to nursery school. Our house was beautiful, with a garden surrounded by a white wall. There were orange trees, red flowers, and scented branches of jasmine climbing up the walls. The house was always full of fruit; when a farmer brought my father his produce he would always leave us two crates of the best fruit, picked with care. I remember the sugar canes as if I were eating them yesterday. I have a fixed image—whether from those days or born of many retellings I do not know—of the courtyard at home where my brothers and I have our arms full of long, fat sugar canes, such as I have never seen since, and we are totally absorbed in nibbling and sucking the juice. It was a game for us and a lot of fun.

Karim, one of my father's employees, a robust, healthy-looking man, used to come every day to pick us up and take us to the sea in a small truck, belonging to the firm. He came afternoons after school and in the morning on holidays. Sometimes he would bring his own children, two little girls and a young boy who were more or less the same age as us. The magic began the moment we arrived at the beach and got out of the car. The boys would go in the water and Karim would teach them to swim and float and not be afraid of the waves. The two little girls and I would remain on the beach, dressed, of course, because little girls could not wear swimsuits. This was a wonderful time for me. I was not interested in bathing—it was enough for me to be playing there with my friends. The beach was almost deserted and it was great fun to run and play in the sand and look at the sea in the distance. I can still close my eyes and see the immense sea, the big waves that both frightened and fascinated me. I would often stand there spellbound and turn my head and shiver at the thought of maybe being out there in the midst. Those moments are unforgettable.

They made a fuss of me and spoiled me at home. Young girls are not normally privileged, but for six years I was the only girl among three boys and I enjoyed special attention. I was always being given presents of lovely clothes. My mother still has a beautiful photo of me in a splendid dreamy outfit in yellow.

A young girl came to help my mother with the domestic chores. She was called Fatma. She was a Shiite; in fact Fatma is a name that the Shiites often give their daughters, since Fatma (or Fatima) was the daughter of the prophet Mohammed and the wife of Ali. Fatma was an important presence in our family. She would arrive every morning and stay until after dinner. She was working to help her parents support a big family, which was why, at age 22, she was not yet married. She was slender with black hair and dark eyes, timid, calm, and attractive. We children could count on her complicity in everything that we were not able to ask of our mother. She was very affectionate with Ihsan, because he was the smallest and so beautiful: she coddled him and spoiled him more than all the rest of us. It was good to have her around and we looked on her as one of the family.

But that wonderful time of prosperity was not to last long.

The Disaster

Explosions, smoke, flames, shrieking, terrified faces. A sudden break in my memory.

It was 1948, but I don't remember exactly which month. In days riots spread across all of Palestine. Gunfire could be heard all over Jaffa. Rockets fell thick and fast during the bombardment, amidst a constant wail of sirens. My father often stayed at home, not saying a word. We no longer went to the beach. It became dangerous even to go to school. The tension in the air was tremendous and I was very frightened. At night we would be woken up by the noise of shooting in the streets, and we slept together in the same room, to give each other courage. Many buildings were on fire; one day the cinema near our house burned down. I can still see it engulfed in flames, people screaming and rushing to put out that enormous fire. I was glued to the window, crying.

I heard macabre stories. I heard of dead people, of terror, fear, and desperation. There was talk of Deir Yassin and other massacres. The village of Deir Yassin had been attacked and more than 250 of its inhabitants—old men, women and children—violated and killed. People were terrified when they spoke of the massacre. Loudspeakers in the streets urged the population to take shelter: "You should leave, take your families far away, we are your friends, we are your leaders, we will help you return to your homes and restore order to the city…" Later we learned that these messages were from Israeli troops who passed themselves off as Arab leaders and were trying to persuade people to evacuate, pretending it was only temporary. Leaflets rained from airplanes: "Go away, leave your houses, or you will come to the same end as Deir Yassin…" The horrible massacre of Deir Yassin had been led by Menachem Begin, who would one day become prime minister of Israel. Begin later wrote, "The massacre was not only justified, but there would not have been a state of Israel without [it]." Indeed, that massacre terrorized the people and drove them from their homes.

One day my father came home distraught and trembling. The story he told was terrible: a group of Zionist soldiers had entered the mosque of Jaffa, which was full of people. One of them had opened fire with a machine gun and killed everyone. My father had so many friends among those people. He was terrified and called on God, but God seemed to be looking the other way.

From then on every gunshot, every flash, frightened us. My brothers and I cried all the time. We asked our mother why the Jews were so evil, why did they want to kill us and take our city. My mother did not know what to answer. Like all the people of Jaffa, she was confused and could not understand what was happening.

I shall never forget the evening we decided to leave Jaffa. It is hammered like a nail into my head. I have heard my mother talk about those times so often. Groups of armed Zionists had burst into many houses nearby, sacking and killing; some families were completely wiped out, young girls raped. We were incapable of defending ourselves, whereas the Israelis were well trained and well armed, stronger than us. My father was panic-stricken. He told my mother to get ready and take only a few things with us. We had to leave— we could not stay in our neighborhood.

We lay down but we couldn't sleep. Shortly before dawn my father loaded the little truck from his company, closed our house and the office, taking with him only the keys and some documents. We left for Kafr Zibad in the hope of finding some calm. My father kept telling my mother that we would only stay there a short time until the situation became clear and Jaffa once more became calm.

The distance between Jaffa and Kafr Zibad is not far, because Palestine is small and it takes very little time to cross from one end to another, but the journey was atrocious. There were terrifying scenes along the way: destruction everywhere, tens of thousands of people walking without knowing where they were going.

We were more fortunate than others because we had a place to stay. Those who did not have our good fortune ended up in refugee camps. What is more, many people in Haifa and Jaffa were driven into the sea by the Zionist soldiers, loaded onto ships, and taken to Lebanon, where huge refugee camps sprang up.

The collective exodus was harrowing: old people were abandoned by the roadside because they couldn't walk any further. In the shade of the olive trees people were dying of hunger, thirst, exhaustion. My father picked up as many people as he could along the way, while there was still room in the truck, until finally the tangle of people made it impossible. We had to take back roads to avoid the groups of Jewish extremists. We arrived at Kafr Zibad exhausted.

We heard stories of what had happened to relatives and friends. One child died at his mother's breast because she had squeezed him too tightly and he had suffocated. Other terror-stricken mothers during a fire or a bombardment had grabbed a pillow thinking they were taking their child and discovered their mistake too late. Tales of desperation: mothers who went mad because they felt responsible for their children's deaths.

Though we did not know it yet, my family, along with thousands of other Palestinian families, had permanently lost our right to return to our city, our home, and our land. A few days later, the state of Israel was proclaimed: a boundary was established between the part occupied by the Jews and the rest of Palestine: it was not permitted to cross that boundary for any reason at all.

My father tried immediately to return to Jaffa to take care of his house and business. It was impossible. The road to Jaffa was blocked. All that was left were the documents, the house and office keys, and the hope of returning. But that day never came. We never heard again from Fatma and from Karim and from our many other friends in Jaffa: we don't know what happened to them. Our hope is that they managed to escape to Lebanon, they must have gotten out somehow. Very few people managed to stay. Many families were divided. I know a married man with six children who was living in the part of Palestine that was proclaimed the state of Israel. He was the *mukhtar* of his village and away on a business trip to Tulkarem. He was not allowed to return, his land was considered the "absentee property" and therefore the property of Israel. Members of his family remained working on that land as laborers. He managed to meet up with his family after twenty years but by then each one had his own life. He was a destroyed man.

We stayed in the country for a while. My mother was pregnant for the sixth time and another baby girl, Iqbal, was born during those months. The situation was quite difficult and this new arrival was one more worry. Even now Iqbal resents it when someone reminds her that she was born in the year of the Nakba, the year of the disaster, as if she could help being born at such an inopportune moment.

After the terror of gunshots and incendiaries, for a while it seemed like a vacation to live in Kafr Zibad. But when the vacation had gone on too long, we began to ask to return to our home, our school, our sea. Our parents took pains to answer us. They may not have wanted to accept that what had befallen us was irreparable. They looked for solutions.

I can remember them speaking in a corner of the room one dawn after the five o'clock prayers. They were making plans and I heard the word "Nablus" repeated and thought maybe it was the name of somebody.

I found out that Nablus was a city when my father greeted us one morning and said that we would soon be leaving. My mother took her earrings, bracelets, necklaces, rings, and all the gold that had been given her on her wedding day, and gave it all to my father. Three weeks later, my father returned and told us that we would leave the day after tomorrow for Nablus, where he had rented a house. I was curious, upset, and afraid.

TWO

Nablus
1948–1959

Surviving the Disaster

We went to Tulkarem by car and from there by coach to Nablus.

After Jerusalem, Nablus is the largest city in the area. It lies between Jabal Aybal and Jabal Girazim, two mountains that had been a hideout for the partisans and are still for the youth of the intifada. Upon our arrival, the noise in the city center was deafening. I found myself in a huge crowd, surrounded by the noise of cars and the wail of ambulances.

A taxi took us up a steep street, along the slopes of Jabal Aybal, where the houses clambered toward the summit, seeking a space between the stones and the thick mountain vegetation. Dumbfounded, I gazed at the mountains, which I was seeing for the first time. The beloved seascape of Jaffa was too far away. The taxi stopped in front of a small villa.

Our apartment was on the top floor. There were two rooms and a kitchen; toilets were outside at the far end of a large open terrace. We looked around in silence. I thought of our home in Jaffa, the garden with its orange trees and their perfume, my well-furnished room full of toys. I am sure everyone was thinking the same thing but no one said a word. My mother silently began to organize our few possessions in this ugly new house: there were mattresses, a kerosene stove, some saucepans and plates. Our life was in terrible shape. My initial feeling upon entering that house was confirmed, and it was even stronger when it came time to start school.

My father, who showed great initiative, had managed to start up his fruit and vegetable business in the markets of Nablus and install a roof over it. His next concern was to send us to school. This did not go so smoothly.

One evening he called me in, together with my three brothers. Turning to them he said: "You three will begin school tomorrow." To me he didn't say anything. I shouted: "And me?" He answered me seriously: "There is no place for you; you must wait; we shall see what can be done."

The city was packed with refugees, masses of them cut off from their homes; there were no schools, houses, food, or clothes. Emergency camps and huts sprang up all over. The number of schoolchildren far exceeded the number of places available in the schools.

My brothers were sent to a private school for boys run by Christian priests. My father had gone to extraordinary lengths to get them enrolled, and my uncle, his older brother who lived in Kafr Zibad, helped him with the fees. I, on the other hand, could not go to school: there were no private schools for girls in the city and there was no room in the public schools. I had to wait a year.

For me this was a tragedy. I suffered as I watched my brothers leave in the morning while I had to stay at home. The following year split shifts were organized and new schools found, but only the first grades were open, so all the children between the ages of six and nine had to attend middle school; the alternative was to stay home. The oldest, at least, were given slightly different exercises. I repeated first grade for a second time. In the end I was at the same level as Ihsan, who was two years younger than me.

This gave me a huge complex. I felt terrible when people said: "Poor girl, she doesn't do well at school. Just think, she is in the same class as her brother who is younger than she." My mother would answer that I had lost time because of the Nakba, but that didn't make me feel better. This terrible affront weighed on me all through my school years and spurred me on to study and get ahead. I began to compete with Ihsan. He was not a good student, but nevertheless he was everyone's darling because he was the youngest son. He would forge his school reports and my father, unaware, would reward him with money, clothes, or new shoes. I was always first or second in my class, but no one took any notice: it was to be expected since I was older and was doing the same class as Ihsan. I almost hated him, and hoped that he would fail. He was the symbol of a great injustice as far as I was concerned.

No one had ever said to me "You should study!" No one had ever celebrated my report card, no one ever gave any importance to the grades I received. I suffered terribly. But I had to suffer in silence because no one had time to listen to such subtle, delicate problems. My father was working 24 hours a day and we saw very little of him; my mother was absorbed in her own thoughts and worries. No one in the family was calm—they all had their difficulties and troubles. And in times like these, the first to pay the price were the girls.

I was always happy to go to school. I felt important there because I did well. School was a long way from home and it was quite a walk to get there. It was very cold in Nablus in winter, and in the early days we didn't have many clothes because we had left them all in the house in Jaffa. I wore a dress with a woolen sweater. I didn't have a coat and my shoes had to last until they were finally in holes.

Shoes were a perpetual problem for me. I had to ask my father if I could have a new pair, but I didn't have the courage to do so because he was always in a bad mood. So when my mother was finally able to speak calmly with him, in one of those rare moments when he was at home, she asked on my behalf. Asking for something has always humiliated me; it is such a tangible sign of dependence and lack of autonomy. When we left the house to go to the market for my shoes, my father stayed a few steps ahead of me. We didn't actually walk together. Every few minutes someone would stop to greet him and chat. I would stand there, alone, in the middle of the street, like a lamppost, waiting until they finished talking. It was torture, particularly because it didn't happen just once or twice, but all the way along the street. In the end, of course, he took me to the shop of a friend of his who had horrible shoes that I didn't like at all. Shoes were important to me because they had to last a long time, and in those days I never had two pairs of shoes at the same time. My father did not understand this, and he saw it as an example of my bad character. In the end I would leave the shop with shoes I disliked and tears in my eyes. When we got home he would say to my mother: "Would you believe it? She didn't like anything! There was nothing she liked in the whole shop!" (It is a fact that my sisters and I do have a passion for shoes.)

The privileges I used to enjoy in Jaffa no longer existed after the 1948 disaster. Instead I experienced the disadvantages of being female.

My older brother, Adnan, who was the genius of the family and my uncle's favorite, had put a roof over the terrace to protect himself from the scorching sun and spent entire days reading and writing in that space reserved for him. He often ate there, alone. I would envy him when I brought him his food. He was privileged because he was the first born, because he was a man, and also because he had a strong, rebellious character and managed to get whatever he wanted.

I, on the other hand, had to help my mother with the household chores after school. There was a lot to do in the house and my mother needed help. My little sisters needed to be watched. The house had to be cleaned and put in order. We slept on thin mattresses stretched out on the floor, and every morning they had to be folded up. It's a very practical system: Palestinian families are numerous and there are always relatives and guests in the house. We cannot fill the houses with beds and so, every evening the mattresses and quilts are arranged on the floor and put away again the next morning.

Mornings, before going to school, I would help my mother prepare breakfast. We would fill big, round dishes with olives, cheese and bread, slices of tomatoes, thyme, oil, vinegar, honey. Everyone would help themselves to food and tea or coffee. At midday we prepared more substantial food: vegetables, meat, and rice, and we would wait to eat until we were all together. In the evening we ate what we wanted—a light meal with the same ingredients as at breakfast.

When we had guests, two days in advance we would begin to prepare the many different dishes: *musakhkhan*, our typical bread dish; a round bowl of onions and spices; chicken stuffed with rice; and other traditional Palestinian food. It was slavery! I hated guests and found the preparation for them excruciating—in my opinion, a negative aspect of Palestinian life, because all this work was done to demonstrate to others our own generosity and prosperity. It was done for appearances that did not make sense to me.

Certain dishes could not be cooked on the kerosene stove in the house and had to be carried to the public ovens. One time we had guests, my mother had prepared *kufta*. I had watched her knead chopped meat with parsley, spices, and onions and spread it in a huge round pan of metal with low edges, a typical saucepan found in every Palestinian house. Desserts are also cooked in it, and it is used to carry all kinds of things on one's head. When all was ready, I had to carry it to the ovens to be cooked. On the way I fell and dropped all the *kufta* on the ground—a disaster. At home, everyone was waiting for me and after a while my brothers were sent to find me. They found me hiding because I did not dare return home and tell them of the trouble I had caused. Naturally I was beaten and my mother had to make do with something else. It was no small loss in those days.

It was difficult for my mother to get used to that house and to the life of Nablus. She was no longer the lively person she had been. She didn't talk much. She no longer told us fables and anecdotes, nor did she speak with her ironic humor. It was difficult to joke. She wasn't friendly anymore and it was not easy for me to talk with her.

Another unexpected grief contributed to her silence. Ziyad, her seventh son, the last-born, a son after so many girls, much loved by my parents who thought he had brought them good luck, fell ill when he was only two years old and died of asphyxiation. I remember returning from school and my mother telling me that Ziyad was dead. We didn't go to the cemetery; everything was done in silence because he was a tiny baby. Day after day our house remained silent as a sign of respect for our little brother.

Windows on the World

Time was passing and we Palestinians were still not able to return to our house and our land. Within the family we often talked about Jaffa—it was always in our hearts and in our conversations. We spoke of it with great nostalgia and bitterness. Each of us had our own memories and our own moments of longing for the things we loved and had had to leave.

Gradually we became aware that we had lost everything. People were in shock for a long time, and unable to absorb their new situation; they did not understand why they had been chased away and robbed of everything. It was like an ugly dream, such a feeling of enormous loss. We had heard about the inhuman treatment of the Jews in World War II, but we wondered why we had to be the ones to pay for horrors committed by others. It was too difficult to accept that everything had been lost in a single moment, that a new state existed in our land, with new people who had never seen Palestine, who did not know its traditions, its language, its land, and its perfumes. The tragedy was too great. I always longed for the happy times we had in Jaffa.

One of the few pleasures of those early years in Nablus was taking the bread to the communal oven. My mother would prepare the dough, kneading it into large round thin molds and then put them into pans. The oven was a huge room with an open mouth full of fire at its end, just like the ovens you find in Italy; the uncooked bread was put on a shining stone rack. When your turn came, the baker took your bread and with a paddle pushed it close to the fiery embers. When it was cooked, he put it in big baskets to cool.

There were always people at the oven and one would have to stand and wait for hours or, if you were lucky, sit on a brick bench. The heat was an inferno, but I really enjoyed it. It was my window on the world; my cinema; my open-air theater. It was full of young girls and we heard all the city gossip. It was a place where we would look at each other. Some men were coarse, others refined, and then there were the women. I would stand apart—my mother had warned me not to talk with anyone—watching and listening to all those stories. Anyone who had a radio and had heard the news would come and tell us all about it. Jokes were told, some of them vulgar or nasty. This forbidden world amused a young and curious girl who was easily excited. It was my moment of magic. I was ten years old, but I felt grown up.

We spent five years in that house. But we were growing and needed more room. So my father rented us a different house, quite a nice one on the main street in the center of Nablus. There were two rooms, a long corridor, a kitchen, a bathroom, and a balcony from which you could see out. Naturally one room, and the one bed, was for our parents. The other, which should have been the living room, was instead always occupied by Adnan. During the day the corridor was the living room and by night it was a bedroom for us children. I preferred sleeping in the kitchen, because it was more private—at least the door could be closed. We children slept on mattresses spread out on the floor.

I was thirteen by then and it was in this new house that my life in Nablus really began. The memory is linked to the presence of my brother. Adnan, who was seventeen, was beginning to get involved in politics. His activity gradually intensified; he was constantly holding secret meetings in the house. He and his friends would shut themselves in his room and stay there arguing for hours. I was fascinated by the forbidden aspect of these meetings.

At first my brother considered me too young for such interests, but as I began to ask more and more questions, he began to tell me the history of Palestine and explain the reasons for all this activity.

In 1947 the United Nations had approved a plan for the division of Palestine, and then in 1948 the state of Israel was established. The area of Palestine, where we had taken refuge, was put under the control of the Jordanian monarchy, as a reward for King Abdullah, who had always collaborated with the English and the Jews in order to keep his own crown.

The Palestinians were not willing to give up the least part of their national territory; they wanted to return to that part of Palestine that had been forcibly taken from them. The loss was too recent. Shortly after 1948, a group of Palestinians shot King Abdullah while he was at prayer in the mosque of al-Aqsa in Jerusalem, killing him. This was a defiance, an act of extraordinary courage against one of those responsible for the Nakba. As a result Jordan created a police regime in the area now known as the West Bank, forbidding any form of cultural or political demonstration. King Hussein, who was extremely young, succeeded King Abdullah and sent a Bedouin army into Transjordan. These desert tribes were extremely loyal to their sovereign. For the Bedouins, the king came first and then God; many of them could not read or write. They were told that all the Palestinians were communists, that they did not believe in God, nor in the family, and that they hated the king. For this reason the Jordanian soldiers were tough on people and beat them up; it was impossible to reason with them; for them the only important thing was to protect the king from the bad Palestinian communists. The Jordanian regime at the time obstructed the construction of industries and a university, yet they used the abilities and professional knowledge of the Palestinians to construct and improve their own country.

1953 was a very heated year in our history. There was political ferment in Nablus and in the whole of the West Bank. Nasser's revolution had just taken place in Egypt. He was the first Arab leader to say to the West, *No more subjugation*; it was he who awakened the soul and the nationalism of the Arab people. In Palestine this was a period of intense secret political activity, a time of the birth of groups and parties.

The Palestinians lived these moments very intensively. They had been let down by their so-called "Arab brothers" who had supported the Palestinians in word only but never in deed. In fact they had collaborated in the Nakba and had used the Palestinian cause to create their own revolutionary image and attract consensus. Nasser was the first Arab leader to criticize the pro-

Western Arab regimes, to challenge the mighty power of America, and to make contact and have a relationship with the Soviet Union. The hopes of many resided in him.

Adnan had joined the Ba'ath party, a secular socialist party that believed in the political and economic union of the Arab world. It was founded by Michel Aflaq, a Syrian Christian. The Palestinians immediately loved this party because it demanded the rights of the Arab peoples and aspired to Arab unity, proposing the distribution of lands and property to those who worked them, the farmers. The Palestinians were aware of their tragedy and asked the Jordanian and other Arab regimes for better social conditions and a more serious effort to make a return to Palestine possible. There was extensive participation in these movements, because the people had profound reasons for struggling.

A great number of Palestinians joined the Ba'ath during that period; it was a strong and very popular party. Of course there were other parties: the communists, the Arab nationalists (ANM, or Harakat al-Qawmiyyin al-Arab), out of which grew the Popular Front for the Liberation of Palestine (PFLP). There was the Party of the Great Syria, a rightist, nationalist party that was interested only in reuniting the fertile triangle zone—that is, Syria, Lebanon, and Palestine. Then there was the Muslim Brotherhood, which was made up of a minority and was supported by the Jordanian authorities. All the other groups were secret.

Tension was always in the air. It was normal to go home and find the house surrounded by police who were searching for a book, a leaflet, a name or telephone number, or whatever else that would prove membership in a party, or a student organization, or some group or other that was engaged in political activity. Sometimes we received warnings of these searches and then I, too, would help to hide the political material in the garden, in the ground, or pass it from house to house across the rooftops. Other times, I would return from school and find the police in front of the house and I would ignore them and walk straight on; it was a very natural reaction, to wish not to be seen by them.

My brother Adnan was arrested more than once, his political involvement was known, evidently; but the Jordanian authorities did not always have proof. Even Issam was involved in politics, especially in the student organization, when strikes and demonstrations were concerned. On those occasions he was hit and beaten—he still suffers back pain from all the beatings he took. Adnan was eventually put under house arrest and that began a really difficult period. It was terrible to have such a lively fellow shut up in the house 24 hours a day: he grew nervous and would explode in anger. But he continued his meetings. The house was always full of people, talking hour after hour, shut up in his room. I worked hard preparing them coffee and tea.

My family soon tired of this situation. My father was worried about survival and for him it was absurd to see this boy ruining himself at his own hands. He couldn't stand so many people in the house, endangering his entire family. But he never said a word. Nor could my mother complain— Adnan would get angry and fight with them. This dramatic situation lasted two years. I was the only person with whom Adnan could talk. He fascinated me: I was bewitched by his deep voice, his blue eyes, and his enormous culture. Very early on I became his pupil, his favorite. I was looked on as his—no one could harm me; only he could yell at me. In this way he encouraged my rebellion and increased the conflict with my parents. This also made my relationship with Issam difficult, despite my great love for him. Of the three boys, Issam was the most reasonable and so bore the weight of the sacrifices needed to keep the peace in our difficult home situation. Ihsan did not help things: he was the youngest and very spoiled. He made no effort at school and gave my father other cause for worry.

Adnan loved to read and write and argue; all of his and Issam's group read extensively; our house was always full of books. I don't think there was a volume published in Lebanon or Syria that did not reach our house. Publishing was very advanced in Lebanon and Syria; many translations of Russian, German, English, and French classics came our way. But always secretly, because it was forbidden to read any texts in which the argument was the slightest bit political. Adnan was interested in philosophical studies and at the time was reading Kant, Hegel, and Sartre. There were books, too, on socialism, Marxism—Gramsci, for example, and Togliatti. The Ba'ath aspired to socialist ideals, but did not apply Marxist analysis to our society. Adnan, on the other hand, declared his Marxist convictions; he was always a little bolder than the others.

Interest in politics forced us to broaden our horizons and learn more; it increased our desire to understand and learn. The Palestinians began to study extensively—this was our passport to life, our means of survival. In the refugee camp near our home, young men could be seen spending the night outside under a blanket, studying under the street lights, because there was neither light nor space in their houses. For them, studying was almost like a piece of land: it offered protection and security. Everyone, *everyone* studied, and kept at it. It was the one thing left to them, now that they had lost everything else.

Adnan began to have me read books and party pamphlets. Often they were typed pages, analyses of the international situation, information and stories about colonialism and imperialism, the Russian revolution; there were directives from national leaders all over the Arab world, comments on party lines and ideologies.

Sometimes I stayed awake until two in the morning, and he read me passages from Nietzsche, Hegel, and Kant, or talked to me about Marx. Of course I didn't understand anything at first, but woe betide me if I yawned. Sometimes I would write short stories of love, morality, political struggle, very innocent things; my heroes were always people involved in politics. Although I didn't realize it at the time, my brother was my hero. I would read him what I had written and he encouraged me. He would scold me if I used inappropriate language.

Whenever Adnan left to go sign in at the police station, I would clean his room. I would stand entranced amid all those books, the smell of cigarettes, the disorder, and the intellectual atmosphere... it was a place of dreams. I couldn't wait to grow up so that I could smoke; I still love the smell of cigarettes, because it reminds me of that magic atmosphere of discussions and political plans, of cultured people, and of books. Instead of cleaning the room I would begin to read.

My brother gave me all the books I wanted. I read American, French, Russian classics—Hemingway, Steinbeck, Maugham, Tolstoy, Gogol, Dostoevsky. I liked Dostoevsky very much, the way he took his time, his details and his analyses of people. I loved Kafka, Camus, and I liked Oscar Wilde. Gandhi and Nehru were among those who gave us our political education and our party. I was like a machine devouring books; I read everything I could find. I also read Arab writers and poets like Taha Hussein, Badr Shaker al-Sayab, Ihsan Abd-al-Quddus, Nizar Qabbani, Tawfiq al-Hakim, and Nagib Mahfouz.

It wasn't enough for me to know only Arab literature; I needed to read other writers outside my world. I searched for experiences that were closer to my way of feeling at that time and I found them in Western writers. Over the last two centuries, the West had a cultural strength that was greater, freer, and more developed, with a greater awareness of philosophical and existential themes. The West seemed more capable of producing ideological analyses and tools, of interpreting reality. Arab literature, on the other hand, was traditional: there were widespread popular novels, with complicated plots, in which everyday life was portrayed as a mesh of typical characters in classic roles, against a background of the political and social situation of the time. Some books had a strong political message but had difficulty confronting the philosophical and existential problems that interested me. Simone de Beauvoir was my gospel. For me she mirrored my experience as a woman, my human and cultural interests. I began to learn about existentialism, which I would have loved to study in depth at the university.

I read all the time and in any situation. I used to cuddle up on the couch that stood in a corner of the kitchen, and hide my book in a textbook and pretend to be studying, I would even tell my mother that I had a test the next day in class. But my mother did not always believe me: she couldn't read or write, but she could tell a novel from a textbook and school was sacred for her. On the rare occasions that I went to the cinema I would take a book with me, not wanting to waste even the intermission. At school I would pretend to have a headache and put my head down on the bench with the book on my knees and read in hiding. Even when I took a bath, I would call Iqbal, my favorite sister, to sit on a stool and read me a book. I even had a bet with myself that I could read a book a day. I assumed that everyone close to me read and I would go to my friends' brothers to see whether they had books that I did not have, so I could swap with them.

It was then that I developed my great passion for classical music. Adnan would listen to the radio at night; I slept in the kitchen next to his room and so was forced to listen. In the beginning it annoyed me, but then it became my nocturnal companion. Since that time classical music has been my consolation. I would imagine a house all my own, with a switch at the entrance that I could flip to fill the house with music as soon as I entered.

Comrades

When I was fifteen and had completed middle school, I officially joined the Ba'ath party. It was quite natural for me to choose this party: I liked its principles, and it was closely bound to Adnan's and to my daily life. I had heard about it since I was little.

To join the Ba'ath party meant having the party membership card, participating in meetings, and being enrolled in the organization. The party was divided into various sections: boys and girls were together in the older section, but in the younger section boys and girls were separated. I was the section head of my cohort and, because of this, participated in the meetings of both the older and the younger groups. I held meetings at school three times a week to discuss issues, to organize a strike or the distribution of leaflets, to spread party propaganda and to find new members. Naturally, everything was secret;

there was a heavy price attached to being found out. I was happy to be a comrade of the bigger boys; living among those who had more experience and confidence made me grow up faster than my peers.

The boys of the party, friends of my brother, were well educated, active, lively, courageous, and helpful. I had a friendly relationship with them—we collaborated and I admired them; I would see them at meetings, but that was the limit of my relationship with them. Between them and the bigger girls, though, there were amorous tales.

Not very many girls were involved in politics, and those that were involved had usually been influenced by a brother, a father, a cousin, or a girlfriend. Some of those who were older than me were very important examples to follow. They were well-educated girls, prepared and tenacious. I learned a lot from them; they gave me books to read on socialism, then we would discuss them and I would take this store of knowledge and experience back to those who were younger than me.

They also talked about the condition of women, but there was very little feminism in the Arab world in the 1950s. It was only later that some particularly emancipated writers, such as Nawal al-Sa'adawi in Egypt or Ghada al-Samman in Syria, made their voices heard. Ghada al-Samman was of middle-class origin and had been educated in the West. She spoke about sex in her books, and explicitly addressed the relationship between a man and a woman, which was scandalous at that time. But these were isolated cases and their voices had no great resonance, especially in the Arab world. There were no mass movements and little news of this kind of rebellion reached Palestine.

Because of the meetings and my activism, a crowd of girls always hung around me at school. The headmistress considered me a disturbing element—she said I was ruining my companions and leading them astray.

There was tall, strong, brown, short-haired Samia who spoke in a loud voice and used the strong language of men. She had a great presence. Her family was famous for being communist but she had had the courage to be a member of the Ba'ath, rebelling against her relations and parents. She was fearless in showing the world who she really was, and she managed to gain her freedom and the respect of others as well. She was an extraordinary young woman, combative, capable of getting to the bottom of things. For me she was a point of reference. I don't know what she did eventually, whether she married or went to America or some Gulf country. Thinking of her makes me very nostalgic. I long to see her again.

Lubna was also politically involved with me, but she was terrorized by a very difficult and authoritarian father. She had so many sisters and just one brother. She was the eldest. Her mother tried to be her daughters' accomplice but she had neither the strength nor the power. Lubna was very beautiful. She would come to the meeting, but was always in fear of her father. We would often get together and talk, and we read so many books and shared many profound experiences. I remember her sad, resigned face when, as soon as she matured, she came to tell me that she had to marry; her parents had arranged a marriage with a man who worked in Kuwait; she loved a different boy, but her love remained secret and fed her imagination. I saw her again when I moved to Kuwait: She had two sons and was still not in love with her husband. But she was a clever woman and used her beauty to get what she wanted from him. She was always talking about sex and tried to teach me. After her husband's death she was active and decisive, learning German and taking charge of her husband's domestic appliance business. She died during the 1991 Gulf War, in a bus that was bombed while she was trying to leave Kuwait.

On entering high school I made an important acquaintance: Ghada, a teacher who had a liking for me. She understood me, but at the same time she would moderate my extremism, reigning in my enthusiasm for everything, suggesting that I should not always be risking everything.

We soon formed a true friendship, which was unusual between a pupil and a teacher. She was progressive and a sympathizer of the Ba'ath party; she came from a very religious family, her father and brothers belonged to the Muslim Brotherhood movement. Her family strongly disapproved of me, they looked on me as a rebel, a *kafira* (heretic), but she was drawn to my need for freedom and my determination to achieve it. This made up for the difference in our ages. We enrolled the same year in the university in Damascus—she wanted to be far from Nablus. She failed one section of the exams, however, and was forced to return to her old life. She didn't last long there—she did not love her family and disliked living in Nablus. She managed instead to go to the United States to pursue her studies.

Ghada would write to me of her problems there—of her loneliness, of her love affairs that ended badly. She was angry with Arab men and the way they behaved with their fellow countrywomen; they would humiliate them, treating them as if they were either loose or old-fashioned. Then she and her Filipino teacher fell madly in love, despite the fact that it was not easy for a Palestinian woman to think of marrying a man who was not of the same origin, and not even Arab. But she did marry him; they were in love and she had the courage to turn her back on conventions.

I saw her with her husband and children one summer when I was passing through Nablus on my way from Kuwait. Our meeting was very moving. She had earned a doctorate in psychology in America, was teaching at the university, and had opened a nursery school. Her family, however, had not come to terms with her marriage. They were ashamed of her and this rejection made her bitter and embarrassed. I comforted her and we tried to laugh together. We have continued writing to each other over the years. She would send me photos of herself and her children so that I could see them grow. We wanted to see each other so much that on one occasion she came from America just to see me, and we met in Florence. She recently died of lung cancer although she never smoked.

The writer Sahar Khalifeh was my fellow student in those years, though we were not actually very friendly at the time. In those days she was not interested in politics, and she seemed strange, so I used to snub her. But she grew up suddenly, which she talks about in one of her books. She became truly great and successful, and achieved many good things. We are friends now; we see each other when she comes to Italy and we have a lot of respect for each other.

My house was always full of girlfriends. My mother couldn't understand it and would ask me: "But what do you talk about with your girlfriends? What do you do with them?" I loved contact with other people and political involvement made that possible. But I also had other kinds of friends, outside of politics. They were young women with family or love problems. I felt somewhat apart from the girls who were upset over sentimental problems; I found them superficial. But it was difficult to talk about personal problems in our families, where there were so many children; we were mostly left to ourselves.

So girlfriends were salvation. We shared warmth and affection, solidarity and understanding.

Maryam had four sisters. Her family was extremely poor and had a very difficult time surviving. Her father was only able to find work one day in ten. Her oldest sister was a seamstress, but did not earn enough. Maryam rebelled; she did not want to remain chained to her humble origins. She wanted to succeed in life at all costs. So she studied and worked hard at school. This made her serious, morose, and difficult to get along with; others would often avoid her. But I managed to have some very deep conversations with her. I recognized that she was intelligent and felt great admiration for her. When she fell ill and failed her final exam, she became very upset and thought her life was finished. I spent a whole week talking with her and in the end convinced her to repeat the exams. She succeeded in finishing school, earned a doctorate in the United States, and now teaches at the university in Bir Zeit. She helped her family and her sister to study. She got where she wanted—all by herself. I saw her again quite a few years ago, when I returned to Palestine for my sister-in-law's death; she had heard of my return and came to find me; she thanked me again for helping her.

I spent many hours with Leila, studying in her garden, which was full of fruit trees. We would exchange confidences in a shady nook, telling each other about our lives. Sometimes she would nap and I would take advantage of the break to read Kafka. Leila belonged to a middle-class family and certainly was not cut out for politics. But I had a really close friendship with her. We would see each other every day and stayed in contact for many years.

With the Wind in My Hair

What worried my parents most was my reputation. We had a particular expression for describing girls who were too free: *ala hall shariha*, or "with loose hair." I always thought it strange that such a lovely image, a young girl with her hair loose in the wind, should be an offensive expression.

At the time my father and my other family members really feared that I would go *ala hall shari* and insisted on my covering my hair with the *mandil*. I refused: I thought it was ugly and it annoyed me, especially in the summer. I used to see women constantly putting it on and taking it off when men who were not members of the family entered or left their house. On one occasion they made a serious attempt to make me wear it. I remember getting furious. I took it, threw it on the ground, and stamped on it, screaming: "I will kill everyone if you make me wear this horrible scarf." And so it was that I never wore the *mandil*; nor did my sisters.

I never was a "loose woman," I have never gone *ala hall shari*, as my father feared, but I have managed to get what I want, to do things that were a little daring and enjoy the wind in my hair. I went to the movies and saw films like *Julius Caesar* and *Gone with the Wind*, even though my father did not allow it. I went on the sly or pretended that it was a school assignment. Once my father found out by accident, and his scolding was truly unforgettable. I found freedom partly by lying and partly by knowing which duties I simply had to fulfill. I had to lie in order to attend political meetings, and even so, I could manage that only after I finished the household chores. And I had to help my mother before I left for school in the morning, which was a really big sacrifice since I would miss the pre-class assembly and school was everything to me. It was there, where I had so many friends and activities, that I felt truly myself.

I continued my work with the Ba'ath party and lived a sort of double life. Political life required a certain cultural preparation, lots of contacts with people, and even a certain amount of courage and recklessness.

A curfew was imposed in response to demonstrations and unrest and the discovery of secret meetings. Everyone had to remain indoors from six in the evening until the next morning. The curfew did not, of course, stop our activities. My friends and I continued to distribute pamphlets, duplicated secretly by our older comrades. In these pamphlets we spoke of our objectives and our struggle to return to the lands that had been taken from us. We protested against the oppression of the Jordanian regime and against the Arab regimes' alliances with the West. We expressed our support for Nasser in his struggle against imperialism and for the construction of a socialist Egypt that was free and diverse.

A handkerchief knotted to the balcony of my house was the signal to my comrades to be ready to distribute pamphlets. The streets were deserted because of the curfew. The old part of Nablus was a typical Arab suq, full of alleys, covered streets, secret passages, shops, houses, arches and staircases, courtyards and rooftops intertwined with each other, and it was easy to hide. The Bedouins patrolled the main streets but were afraid to venture into the narrow alleys; they feared that people might attack them by throwing objects out the windows. Today these little streets drive the Israelis mad; they barricade them with huge blocks of reinforced concrete in order to hamper the intifada. Nablus is still called *jabal an-nar* (mountain of fire) because it has always been the starting-point for revolts and riots.

One night, while my parents were asleep, I went with one of my comrades to the house of a young party member. My sister Iqbal, who adored me and would do anything for me, covered my escape; she stayed up all night to open the window for me on my return. I was torn between fear of the Jordanian soldiers and dread of a violent reaction from my father. We dug up the pamphlets from the garden and hid them under our clothes; it was not difficult for us women, because no one would be allowed to search under the skirt of a young girl. Jumping from one alley to the other, from one house to another, we managed to put the pamphlets under the store shutters, and beneath the doors of the houses. It was important for people to find our messages in the morning. The police surrounded the schools, preventing us from approaching and entering. The dark was helpful and the narrow streets and secret passages protected us. By chance one of our comrades, on guard at a post in the open, was stopped by the soldiers, beaten up, and arrested. The rest of us managed to hide in a dark corner behind a garbage can under the stairs of a house, where we had to spend the entire night. It was a disaster: our parents thought we were at home, but of course we could not risk being taken by the Jordanian soldiers.

Dawn brought us some relief. The curfew was over and we were able to head for home. Everywhere was enveloped in silence. I knocked quietly at the window and Iqbal, who had stayed awake all night, anxious about my safety, leaped to her feet and ran to open it. I quickly threw on my pajamas over my clothes and jumped into bed. When my mother came to wake us at seven, she found me in my bed. She had no idea of my nocturnal adventure.

That year of 1955 the West Bank saw a wave of protests and demonstrations in which I participated. Iraq, Turkey, England, and Iran had formed an alliance that came to be called the Baghdad Pact. Iraq in those days was ruled by a puppet monarchy created (of course) by the British. The prime minister, Nuri Said, was a small man, with an evil look, like Shamir. Then there was the Shah of Iran, who was the United States' man, the man of the West. The pact was formed to protect Israel and to check some of the Arab countries, primarily Nasser's Egypt, which had come under the influence of the Soviet Union, and Syria, where there was strong nationalist ferment.

The Baghdad Pact countries also tried to convince Jordan to adhere to their alliance and King Hussein was taking this matter under consideration. We Palestinians were furious because we knew that this was one more way of strangling us, for Israel's benefit. One more way of putting an end to our dream of returning to Palestine.

At a meeting of student representatives it was decided not to demonstrate for reasons of safety. I disagreed totally and did not want to adhere to the decision of the older students. I went back to my school and called a meeting of my comrades at which I told them what had happened and what I thought. We were all in agreement that the demonstration should take place and that we, the students of the third grade in middle school, could decide without the consensus of the older students. We organized a strike for the following day and included the other girls' schools around us.

We mobilized all our forces and went out and demonstrated. It was the first time that Nablus had ever seen an all-female procession. All the middle school and younger students came out; the older students remained in school because they were obviously not ready to take their lead from younger girls. The procession began to file past the curious and astounded people. I put myself at the head of the procession to incite my comrades and feed the fire of rebellion. I shouted slogans and worked at keeping up the morale. I felt responsible for the initiative and did not want the demonstration to fail. Our goal was to reach the British consulate and tear down the flag. The consulate was at the other end of the city and that meant crossing the whole of Nablus on foot.

My house was ahead of us on the main street. By now I could see it in the distance and thought of my mother's reaction when she saw me from the window. I was assailed by fear: My father would not think twice about slapping me in front of everyone. I made myself as small as possible, lowered my head, and hid myself among my comrades. Fortunately, I escaped my parents' eyes. A lion turned into a lamb!

But as soon as we had left my house behind, there I was again in the heat of the demonstration, taking up my role, feeling a sense of myself. I was very proud because the procession was long, successful, and advancing. Of course the police, King Hussein's Bedouins, surrounded us the whole time. When we arrived at the Consulate, we hurled ourselves en masse at the British flag. We snatched it down, tore it up, and threw it away. Then we were enveloped in tear gas. We called to each other by name. When we heard gunshots, we ran. Then I don't remember any more.

I woke up in hospital with a leg wound. The girls' demonstration had ended in a tragedy. One of my comrades had been killed, hit by the soldiers' bullets; another of my friends had to have a leg amputated. I felt rage, grief, and desperation. I thought that my guardian angel had protected me.

Many, many students from school came to see me, to show their support for me and solidarity for our courageous demonstration. My mother, of course, also came, this soldier, this horse, this rock, who never said a tender word, who disliked my activity and was naturally very angry. She yelled at me because my lovely new blue velvet suit with white cuffs and collar was torn and burned and—as if that was not enough—I had lost the scarf.

I was surprised to see that my mother had tears in her eyes despite her angry tone. "You deserve what has happened to you, because you meddled in affairs bigger than you. You have been reckless and irrational." Meanwhile she went on drying her eyes. I couldn't believe that she was crying for me.

I discovered afterward that her tears were the result of the tear gas that impregnated my clothes. Still, it was comical, her tough tone and the tears streaming down her face.

I remained in the hospital for forty days and when I returned to school my comrades and some of the teachers made a fuss of me. I was very proud of what I had done. As for my wound, it still bothers me thirty years later. I had to have another operation because some of the shrapnel was still embedded in my leg. Even now, my leg sometimes swells. And it was not the last time that my political activity caused conflict with my family.

Egypt had always been considered the cradle of Arab culture. In Cairo there were great universities: al-Azhar, the university for Muslims; 'Ain Shams; the American University. Cairo offered many more possibilities for study and work than Syria or Jordan.

And after the July Revolution of 1952, there was that great big person who resembled the statue of a pharaoh, who had brought a new model to Arab politics. He was very big; he was a giant. We called him *Abul-Hul* (the Sphinx). We Ba'athisti supported Gamal Abdul Nasser because he wanted to bring about socialism and economic and political unity to the Arab world. He wanted to free the Arab spirit and rouse the people, and he was succeeding.

Nasser was, at that time, the greatest supporter of the Palestinian cause. The Egyptian revolution against Farouq had been carried out by Nasser and a group of officials driven by their disappointment over the treachery of King Farouq toward the Palestinians in 1948. Farouq, who was a pawn of the British, had sent his soldiers to fight for Palestine with out-of-date ammunition and guns abandoned by the British after World War I. Nasser understood then that the Arab "liberation" of Palestine was a complete farce. Since then, Nasser supported the Palestinian cause. (In fact, it was during his rule that the first attempt to create a Palestinian organization came about. The Palestinian Liberation Organization (PLO) was founded by Ahmad Shuqairi, a Palestinian living in Egypt. Shuqairi was one of those religious people of noble origin who did not understand politics in revolutionary or popular terms, and so this organization was not particularly successful. But in 1969 Yasir Arafat took over the leadership, and the PLO became what it is today.)

We Palestinians loved Nasser in return. During his long, seemingly endless, speeches on the radio, every city, village, and street was deserted. Everyone stayed indoors to listen. Later, in Italy, I saw that it was the same with the national party there. Nasser improvised his speeches; he was ironic (something the Egyptians also had in common with the Neapolitans). He would tell jokes and make fun of King Hussein, calling him "the little king" because of his short stature. He poked fun at all the corrupt Arab leaders. His speeches were transmitted by a Cairo station called Sawt al-'Arab, the Voice of the Arabs. The Jordanian government had forbidden us to listen to Nasser's speeches, but everyone listened to them all the same: there wasn't a house or a store that did not have the radio turned up to full volume. People left their windows open as a challenge to the Jordanian soldiers. Nasser's voice resounded everywhere, so that the police did not know what to do. They would have liked to arrest the whole nation.

The radio was the freest source of news. People also listened to Radio London and Sawt Amerika (Voice of America), an American radio station that transmitted, and still transmits, in Arabic. We could hear from these sources that the West hated Nasser. He was attacked every day; it seemed he was the most wicked man in the world. But this has always been a typical Western attitude. As soon as any Arab leader tries to raise his head, the West tries to destroy him, calling him a madman, a crazy, a dictator.

When Nasser nationalized the Suez Canal in 1956, he lit a fire in the heart of every Palestinian. (Something similar happened in 1991 when Saddam Hussein's Iraq was attacked by an international coalition under the aegis of the United Nations.) Nasser called on Arabs to lift up our heads and be free. He called for Arab unity, for an end to submission to the West. His was a great challenge. Nasser was right, we felt: It was not fair that foreign companies charged for ships to pass through Egyptian territory,

territory that was considered free. It was ridiculous. The fact that the Suez Canal had been built by the English and the French didn't mean anything.

Faced with Nasser's action, the West went crazy: England, France, and Israel attacked Egypt and occupied the Sinai. Obviously at the center of this was Israel, which is always opposed to any possibility of Arab unity, of Arab awakening, of any movement in the direction of self-determination by the Arab people. This war shook the hearts of all Palestinians and all Arabs.

Demonstrations began. I started collecting money in support of Egypt to purchase weapons of defense against this aggression. I remember in school each of us would remove our rings and earrings to sell them, or take our savings to send to Nasser.

I was in high school at the time. We went as a delegation to the post office to send Nasser a telegram that said we were ready to do anything, even go fight. We were, admittedly, somewhat naïve: Unquestionably, that telegram never arrived at its destination, but remained on the desk of some Jordanian official. But we had done it with the typical enthusiasm of youth. We went back to school and pinned the receipt for the telegram on the wall, as if we had won the war.

One day the Bedouin soldiers who were on guard at the school entered the building and found pamphlets all over the place, in the bathrooms, in the classrooms, in the director's office. The director, who knew about my activities, sent for me and sent a janitor to open my bag. It was full of pamphlets. The director, I suppose, had no particular political stance: she simply didn't want problems in the school. So she handed me over to the police.

As always at times like these, I was terrified of my parents' reaction—particularly my father's—so I gave the police the name of a cousin who had always protected and helped me. On this occasion he came to the police headquarters and paid the fine. He was a simple fellow, not very educated, and he had never been concerned about politics, so he was completely confused by the fact that a girl could be arrested and interrogated, and that she had to pay a fine to be let go. He gave me a good-natured lecture on the honor of a young girl and of her family, and then he took me home.

Unfortunately, I was expelled from school and that notice could not be kept hidden from my father. I went home and hid behind a couch, where I stayed for 24 hours, while everyone told my father that I had stayed at my cousin's. I heard my father shouting and saying I had too much freedom. My cousin tried to defend me but my father was in a rage. I feared that I was utterly ruined. But I was not the only one to be expelled, and I knew that being expelled for political reasons would stir up a reaction among the students. Indeed, soon there were other strikes and demonstrations, and students refused to do their homework. After about three weeks we were all readmitted.

Men and Women

While my brother Adnan was under house arrest, several young women in the party played truant from school to attend the meetings at our house. This was a much too serious action for our times—almost a scandal—and it put my family at risk.

I suspect that they were all in love with Adnan. It was so easy to fall in love with him. The meetings themselves had the attraction of being forbidden, and Adnan, with his blue eyes, talking and talking in his deep voice, stroking his blond moustache, a cigarette always in his hand, was almost irresistible. He was their teacher, their idol. He suggested reading, taught them to think, to rebel, to take part in politics, and he answered their doubts and their questions. Adnan knew how to appreciate them; he knew how to find something extraordinary in each one of them. And he wasn't telling lies—there really was something special in each one of them: simplicity in one, in another rebellion, in another beauty. He told them all he loved them, and so he conquered them, deluded them, and made them suffer. That was the way he was. For him it was almost a crime to love only one woman. "They are all so marvelous," he would say. "How can one love just one woman only?"

Once I forgot to knock before opening the door to his room, and I found him kissing one of my girlfriends. This, when the day before he had given me a love letter to give to another girl! I was uncomfortable and blushed, as if the kisses were who knows what. I thought his way of behaving was a terrible contradiction, a huge hypocrisy. I was their go-between—so much so that my mother had nicknamed me "telephone"—and I felt torn between refusing to participate in this deception and the impossibility of telling my friends what I knew.

I was fifteen and very idealistic, and this deception colored my perception of men. I became convinced that even the best of them were not to be trusted and that one should keep one's distance from them.

In those days there was a young man who was in love with me. He followed me like a shadow, sent messages by way of my younger sister, and dedicated songs to me on the radio. I thought all of this was stupid. Love couldn't be, shouldn't be, like that. Nevertheless, I got used to being followed and, when he wasn't there, I would look for him. His letters were very beautiful, pages and pages in which he praised me. He said I was always in his thoughts, and that he took note of everything I did. The things all lovers say. When I noticed that he was downstairs, I pretended not to see him and walked in front of the window, so that he could see me; at other times I arranged for him to see me tearing up his letters. He aroused my feminine pride— I too could talk about love and letters with the other girls.

But I was neither fascinated, nor in love.

One day as I was returning from school he came running to meet me and, pretending to bump into me, gave me an embrace. I found myself trembling in his arms, his face red with emotion brushing against mine. I was frightened. I ran home indignant. I told Ihsan, the youngest and most delinquent of my brothers. He went in search of him with his friends, beat him up, and told him to get lost. I did not want to hear from him again.

This episode increased my distrust of men and my desire for a love based on deep knowledge and real understanding. I could not accept the idea of an arranged marriage, which my parents were beginning to suggest. By then I was getting older. I had begun to menstruate and my breasts were developing. My parents thought me a rebel because of my political activity and my behavior. They said I had lost my head and that Adnan was spoiling me, and they did everything they could to remove me from his influence.

My mother found me one day talking in the street with a party comrade of Ihsan's, and afterward I had to undergo a sort of family trial. Elderly aunts added their dose of scoldings, which rained down on me from all quarters: "Enough of it with this child, it's time she were married, it's time for her to cover her head. Salwa is mature now, she has learned how to read and write and has finished the Qur'an—why does she need to continue going to school?" (We finished reading the Qur'an in the third grade of middle school.) "She has studied enough now and has gone far enough. There is someone waiting who has asked for her hand. He should not be put off." At sixteen a young girl was considered ready for marriage. I hated these aunts who came and stirred up trouble.

There were actually cousins who were courting me and had their eyes on me. I was the oldest girl in the family and it was permitted to marry cousins. Their father was someone big in the Ministry of Public Education—an important, cultured man, who had written history books, someone who had made his own way. They were roughly my age and had been given a very liberal education, they had had the chance to travel, and were permitted to drink and to have fiancées. They used to come to our house all dressed up, their hair combed like James Dean's. In those days, even we followed the American fashions of the 1950s. We girls wore tight-waisted dresses with bell-shaped skirts that swayed when we turned. The dresses were quite short but, of course, never low-cut. I felt the same way about these cousins as I had about my unfortunate suitor: I was ambivalently attracted to them. When they came to visit I would dress up and flirt, but I still dreamed of a less superficial love and rejected the idea of marriage.

I kept telling my parents that I would rather kill myself than get married. I had so many plans! Studying was my sole aim in life. I was involved politically, I felt free, and had no intention of putting an end to my future by going and marrying someone I didn't like.

My parent's efforts failed in the end, partly because of my insistence, and partly because they themselves were not really convinced that marriage was the best thing for me. They faced and resolved the conflict between their mental attitude that bound them to tradition, and their curiosity, their imagination, which kept them open to new solutions in life. Despite what felt then like a lack of understanding, I am aware that my parents provided a great example for me and for all my brothers.

My Father

After the disaster of 1948, it was a daily struggle for my father to meet his family's needs. Like others of his generation, his back had been broken by this great tragedy, but he was determined to start over.

He couldn't understand the politics of the younger generation; his own resistance against the British had been a spontaneous struggle. Our way of doing politics, on the other hand, was organized, more ideological, and rich in words and ideals. For him, though, these politics meant his children being beaten, imprisoned, and expelled from school; it meant having the police always at his house, jeopardizing the safety of our whole family, which became labeled as Ba'athist. He was always involved with the Jordanian authorities, asking for favors or giving presents to King Hussein's secret service, in order to get us out of trouble. His life was hard enough without this added difficulty. It didn't make sense to him to challenge the government and bring all that extra suffering into the house.

His generation had lost hope. But it was precisely because we had seen the desperation and deception that people like my father had suffered that my generation became so combative.

I felt such tenderness for that bronzed face with the green eyes staring out, framed by the white *hatta*, always in his traditional Palestinian dress, long pants with a jacket on top. But I was never able to communicate with him— I couldn't even call him "papa." I was never able to find a topic of conversation. I loved him so very much, but he was distant, absorbed in the problems of survival.

He was always working and making sacrifices for us. In the end, around 1958, he managed to buy a piece of land on the outskirts of Nablus, close to the refugee camp of Balata, and began to build a big house. It was in a somewhat isolated area, along a street that came to be called "the street of love." Not many people lived on that street—just a few houses and no street lights—so it was a place to go where you would not be seen.

Our "villa" was very big—two stories high, with marble floors and large verandas and a garden. My father placed the keys of the Jaffa house in the best spot in the living room. He still dreamed of returning, even though he had managed to rebuild a life. He longed for our old house, and also for the sea and the fields of oranges and grapefruits. He never stopped flirting with the idea of creating another citrus grove in Palestine.

One day he bought another piece of land and did, in fact, create a small paradise: He planted orange, lemon, and grapefruit trees, built a little house with two rooms, and put in a large basin of water—something like a swimming-pool. Despite his age, every day, after work, he went and watered his fruit trees. Instead of digging trenches for the water, he installed rubber tubes with a little spigot by every plant. With his ingenuity alone, he had invented a modern system of irrigation. His trees grew well and were all the same height. Their blooms were marvelous with a strong perfume. He was as proud of them as if they were the finest creations of his life. I remember that field with the high blue sky far overhead and the faint white markings of the clouds. I remember the colors and the perfumes.

That piece of land was close to the Israeli border, so no one, not even a guard, could stay there. At night, Israeli soldiers crossed the border and stole oranges and lemons. This was the sort of contact we had with the Israelis in those years. They were an invisible but palpable presence beyond that absurd frontier. Many people had property a few dozen meters over the border; it was unreachable.

We still have that citrus grove in Palestine and even though these days it costs a lot to maintain it, we all cling to it. It represents the tenacity, affection, and love of our father.

My father was a great dreamer and in order to realize his dreams he always took risks and managed to achieve even bigger things. He gave us a beautiful and comfortable home and a green field perfumed with oranges and grapefruit. He managed to send all nine of his children to university, without ever suggesting that studying was only for men and not women. In this he was truly great.

My Mother

I used to fight constantly with my mother during my school years because she did not share my political commitment. It was not women's work, she said. She wanted me to be a normal girl who took care of her younger brothers and helped clean the house and do the laundry. When my father got angry with my brothers, she protected them and blamed the girls instead, directing all his tension toward me. The idea was too deeply rooted in her that boys and men had a right to greater freedom of action and movement. She also did not want to create even greater conflict between my father and his sons.

My mother led a very traditional life, full of deprivations, focused entirely on her husband and her sons, without any personal dimension. She never left the house; she would wait for her husband to come home and listen to him venting his frustrations. He could say anything he wanted to her, it was a man's right to lose his temper and even to yell; it happened in every family. But she would answer back and never suppress her own opinions.

It used to be, and still is, a Palestinian custom that when a conflict arose between husband and wife, the woman would go to her parents' house. It was her way of protesting and indicating her disagreement, her way of seeking help and the protection of her own family. But it was also a two-edged sword. If all went well, the husband would leave her there for several days and then would fetch her home victorious. On the other hand, sometimes to teach her a lesson, the husband would leave his wife there for several months, which inevitably forced her to return shamed and more docile than before. My mother never resorted to this custom: there were problems, of course, but she would resolve them for herself. She thought that no one could help her; no one else could understand the nuances of her relationship with her husband. She was a proud, haughty woman who had a high opinion of her own ability and her own self-sufficiency.

She was of country origin and was proud of it. Country people in our land had a different way of talking than city folk. She had lived in the country until she married at the age of fourteen and moved to Jaffa. She could have changed her accent. It would have been one way to gain access into that new society. But she always refused to do it; she considered it a falsification of identity. She said she wanted to present herself for what she was and, if others didn't accept her, then she could do without them.

My sister Rima was born during the week in which school began. I was in the house that day waiting for my father, who had gone to buy our new books and notebooks. It was a holiday and I was excited about the start of a new year. When I heard my mother calling, "Salwa, Salwa, come, come," I didn't think it was anything important and didn't pay attention. She had a great big stomach, but just like always in the last months of pregnancy. I didn't go to her, and she had to give birth alone. She took a ladder, climbed up into the attic and took down the clothes that were ready for the newborn. She climbed down with the case of clothes, lay down on her bed and gave birth to the little girl alone, without a murmur. She called me afterward to go bury the placenta in the garden; by then, the baby was already born and lying close by her in a basket. My father learned of Rima's birth that evening when he returned home. My mother had a strength and an independence that at times seemed almost too much.

During my last year of high school, our last sister, Nadia, was born. Badia had been born two years before. Nadia's birth offended me; I felt ashamed. My mother kept giving birth to children—a constant, uncontrolled production. I thought it was absurd. We were already five sisters, three brothers, and one little brother who had died. There I was, finishing high school, and my mother gave birth to another little girl. I was ashamed in front of my friends and my party comrades. By then we understood that it was not sensible to go on making children in this way, that it limited the freedom of women. In our meetings we had often talked about the problem of birth control. Then, too, my mother was of a certain age, but she and my father hoped to have another son. This made the situation even more unacceptable for me.

For my parents, however, Nadia's birth was always considered good fortune. From that day on, my father's business began to improve. He succeeded in finishing the villa and the atmosphere in our family grew more relaxed. My parents have always had a special love for this daughter, whom they nicknamed *bitjib al-haz* (good luck).

She was always in my father's arms. Her relationship with my parents is different from mine. When we talk about them, it is almost as if they aren't the same people.

My parents have always been very religious; not a day has gone by that they have not said their prayers five times. But their religiosity is of a particularly attractive kind. Instead of praying in traditional fashion, they actually hold a dialogue with God. I used to listen to the prayer in the silence of the house at five o'clock in the morning. "But God, you who are in heaven, why do you do this? Why have you let the Jews chase us out of our homes? Why have you defeated us?"

My mother used to actually argue and settle her account with God, scold him and ask him: "Why do you do this or why do you do that?" When she would begin to talk with God and scold him, my brothers would hide behind the door and listen to her, because she made us laugh.

This sort of behavior was her very own rather than a characteristic of Islam, even though it is said that in Islam the relationship with God is direct since it does not rely on the mediation of a priest. But in Islam, the relationship with God also involves reading the Qur'an and repeating from memory its words. Instead, my mother—who had never studied—kept an open, innovative mind, and her religiosity was neither blind nor rigid.

I remember something splendid. Palestinian women when they pray must put on a long skirt that covers their legs down to their feet. My mother, who usually wore clothes that came just below her knee, said it was a waste to make a skirt with so much material just to pray. That was how she came to invent legwarmers! She sewed a sort of stocking that covered the leg from where the skirt ended to the feet. It was funny, ridiculous, revolutionary. We would all go to look at our mother presenting herself before God in these pantaloons! It was very strange, too different. She would say: "God understands, God does not like appearances, God told us to cover our legs, not put on a skirt."

All this helped me to experience religion in a way that was not oppressive, formal, or superficial. Praying was a part of my parents' way of being—it was their security, their hope. If it was an illusion, I never thought to question it because it made them happy. Of course my mother would scold us: why did we not pray, why did we not respect Ramadan, why did we not read the Qur'an. She told us we could not be happy if we did not obey God's laws, but she did not insist. Later in life, when we were grown up, we would often joke with her about these things. Because of the unusual religious education I received from my parents, I have always looked on religion and my relationship with God as something exclusively personal. This also made me appreciate the fact that the Ba'ath party was secular.

Despite her apparent submission, my mother was a strong woman who managed to influence my father in the most important decisions of life. She had never gone to school and that displeased her, since she understood the great importance of studying. This helped her overcome her own reluctance when I wanted to enroll in the university. Like my father, she was torn between deeply-rooted tradition and the need to adapt to the times and to the requests of her unruly and innovative children.

On the other hand, my mother was also a very generous and sensitive woman. I remember one day, when she was looking out the window, she saw an old man pulling a cart full of cucumbers. At a certain point the little old man slipped and all the cucumbers rolled to the ground. Even though my mother never had much money (my father took care of expenses and purchases), upon seeing the poor old man begin to cry, she took all the money she had and gave it to him, and then helped him pick up the few cucumbers that remained intact. She had a big heart. When our own economic situation improved, she worked hard to help the women in the refugee camps who had a difficult time surviving.

Desire for Freedom

Adnan and Issam did brilliantly on their finals. My uncle suggested to Adnan, who had always been his favorite, that he continue his studies in America, but my uncle died and it was no longer possible. So Adnan went to teach first grade in Jerusalem and then to Irbid in the north of Jordan, where he stayed during the week. At the same time, he enrolled in law school in Damascus, but only went there to take the exams. He studied very little but was nevertheless successful; university was a game for him. Issam also was very smart, but he was over-shadowed by Adnan's dominant personality, as we all were. He was in a hurry to become independent and leave home. He sat for his final exams a year early, squeezing two years into one by studying privately. He found work as a teacher in an elementary school in a town near Nablus; but wanted something more and felt sacrificed. During that time he wore a pathetic suffering look, like one of Stendhal's characters.

When I was eighteen and finishing high school, Adnan went to Kuwait. Kuwait was a new country with enormous economic possibilities. It needed everything: engineers and workmen to build streets and cities, teachers for the schools, and lawyers to make laws. In Palestine, on the other hand, there were no industries, no work—just an enormous supply of ability at all levels. To go to Kuwait became the goal of many Palestinians, who left to work there in the tens of thousands.

After he left, I felt abandoned—cut off from the outside world. Most of all I lacked the spiritual sustenance of books. Until then all kinds of books had found their way to our house. But now that Adnan had moved to Kuwait, none of them came anymore. I would arrange secret assignations to exchange books with my friends' cousins or brothers, or I would send my brother Ihsan to borrow them from the stores in the old city, because it was easier for him to move around. I made a pact with him: in exchange for this favor, I would cover for him when he went to Ramallah to have a good time and returned home late. I continued to devour books and for a period my great passion was for adventure and detective stories. I read Emilio Salgari and Edgar Allan Poe. I loved characters like Rocambole, Arsenio Lupin, and Sherlock Holmes.

I was in my final year of high school—that decisive year that I had looked forward to for so long. The maturità seemed the only way to become a part of a new, more open world. I dreamed about enjoying life at the university, of living alone, making new friends, a whole new existence, a more mature struggle, a more independent life based on my own strength and ability.

Issam had followed Adnan to Kuwait and now I felt

alone at home. I could not stand my family's control and did not want to do any of the things my mother asked of me. I too wanted to leave and discover the world and life. I buried myself in the works of Sartre and Simone de Beauvoir. It was a period of calm in Jordan with less intense political activity. I cut back on my involvement because it was so important to me to finish the school year without any big problems.

I revealed my wish to go to the university in Damascus and my father said he would send me to study medicine or pharmacy—those were the only important faculties. I remember him saying this once in front of relatives and friends. I was happy: it did not matter to me what I would study—the important thing was to leave home and change my life.

Graduation day arrived with a ceremony in which the Queen Mother, King Hussein's mother, would participate. For her it was an act of beneficence, but for me, having to curtsy in front of her was a humiliation. I tried to make myself sick, but didn't succeed, so I made the only curtsy of my life and accepted my diploma.

Once my final exams were behind me, my father reneged on all his promises and said he did not want to send his daughter to live alone in a distant country—it was dangerous and not befitting the honor of a young girl. He was afraid that I would go around *'ala hall shariha.*

It was not easy to get him to change his mind. He could decide my destiny. I did not have enough money to leave without his permission and, moreover, I needed a passport and other documents that I could not get without him. The law in many Arab countries says that a woman cannot have a passport without the consent of her father, her brother, or her husband. It is so cruel when someone else decides your destiny. Faced with my father's refusal, I went on the first hunger strike of my life. I remained three days without eating. My father ignored me. My sisters begged my mother to convince my father to let me go to the university. My mother thought my attitude was a bit foolish, but she understood my desire and had never thought that a woman was any less than a man. The hunger strike didn't work. I began to eat again, but fell into a state of deep discomfort and great sadness. A world, a dream, a wonderful undertaking had collapsed.

My sadness and my renewed insistence finally moved my father, who suggested I enter a women's college, the Dar al-Mu'allimat, a teachers' college in Ramallah. It was considered a privilege to enter that school—the young women who attended learned the only profession permitted women, that of teacher. My uncle in the Ministry of Public Education managed to obtain a place for me even though the school year had already begun.

Ramallah is a very beautiful city, very bright and luminous, in the flat open countryside that is a vacation area for many people. Many Christians lived there and it was an affluent, sophisticated center, full of entertainment. The college was a huge building like a castle, with a gigantic portico, surrounded by a garden full of trees. My curiosity was roused by this new exclusively feminine world, attended by young Christian and Muslim women who came from diverse social situations, and from all parts of what remained of Palestine, from Gaza and from Jordan.

The education followed the English model: There was time for tea and for dancing, and a library for studying. They described it as a refined education for young women, but I recognized it immediately as a gilded prison. My companions had no interests; they lived enclosed in their luxurious cage and thought only of their amorous problems, secret loves that would never be crowned with a true union, because free relationships were forbidden. It was natural that love affairs would develop among women living in such isolation and needing affection. A few girls were interested in politics and culture, but there was no opportunity for discussion or action.

I did not want to spend two years of my life stifled in a sort of English salon, among women who gradually slipped into depression and apathy. I told my father this, but he just thought it proved that I did not really want to study. So I asked my brother Adnan for help. I wrote him a very moving letter in which I told him (even though it was not true) that I had already left the Dar al-Mu'allimat, that I passed my time gazing out the window at home and that I felt like a frustrated housewife. I lied because I did not want him to try to persuade me to continue at the college. He answered me immediately with a thoughtful letter; then he wrote to my father and sent him a plane ticket for me to go to Kuwait. Of course I was extremely happy.

My father agreed because he knew my brothers would watch over me. Appearances were saved, in the eyes of friends and relatives—he was not sending his daughter *'ala hall shariha*, not throwing her into the fray. I went to Amman with my father. Those were a strange three days, because I was not used to being alone with him. I got my passport. My father took me to the airport and finally I left for Kuwait. It was the end of 1959. I was barely nineteen and I had taken my first journey. I felt free and alive, mistress of the world, eager to accomplish all my dreams.

THREE

Kuwait
1959–1966

Arrival

I was in the air. I was flying for the first time. I was happy. I flew with a joyous feeling of freedom. Euphoria. Finally I had done it. I was free from my parents' control. Nablus receded and the horizons widened. New people awaited me, new experiences, a new world.

The plane landed in Kuwait. The doors opened and I was enveloped in a suffocating heat. Sweat was pouring down me. Gusts of wind filled my eyes with sand as I looked around in search of my brother. There was almost a delegation waiting for me. Issam and Adnan were there with many of their friends who had heard talk of me and wanted to come meet me. They were all men, which was embarrassing.

We drove down a long straight street in a huge American car, under a red sky that seemed to envelop us and make us aware of the roundness of the earth. We arrived at a district of square white villas and buildings set well apart from one another. A muffled silence weighed on everything, as if all the energy of the people living there were spent in the effort of breathing in the suffocating air.

I entered Adnan's house. On the floor, on the table, on the shelves, scattered everywhere, were mountains of classical music records. I had never seen so many. They belonged to Ibrahim, a young man from an important Palestinian family who was then living with my brothers. They introduced him to me: he was extremely tall and thin, full of pimples and with a half-closed eye. His presence was disturbing. He spoke little and didn't seem bad, but he made me feel awkward.

Adnan's was a big house: three bedrooms, a living room, kitchen, and bath. It was bare, basic like Palestinian houses. A cook had prepared an excellent meal. I did not sleep in their house, because there was no room for me. I stayed with a couple who were friends of Adnan.

In that newborn country with its extremely closed society, there were no hotels where a young girl could stay alone. But Adnan's thoughtful gesture had a different meaning. By making the decision and finding that place for me to live, it meant once again that I was under his wing, as if I were his property. My hosts were kind—perhaps too kind. I felt somewhat suffocated. I wanted to be freer and have more space for myself. The head of the house was a Palestinian from Gaza who had lived in Damascus, and now had a good position in Kuwait; his wife was Syrian.

Their house was on the beach. It was the first time that I had seen the sea since I left Jaffa, but the sea I remembered was gentler and smoother, more fascinating. Everything around me now was deserted; there was no sign of life; the sand was scalding hot and I couldn't walk with bare feet. The sea was black by night, and in this desert the noise of the water frightened me. The humidity was terrible. Every time I poked my nose outside the door, I felt the need to take a shower. The air-conditioning in the house was on 24 hours a day, and its loud noise gave me a headache.

Politics and Society

When I arrived in Kuwait, it had just come into existence as an independent state; oil had been discovered shortly before. This brought enormous wealth, though it was not strictly the property of the emir of Kuwait. When the West divided up the Arab world and cut this piece of land out of Iraq, it chose two Bedouin tribes, the Sabbah and the Jabir, and cut a deal. In exchange for being agents of the West, they would become very rich. The same families still govern Kuwait today.

Palestinians made up the majority of immigrants in Kuwait. The first to arrive were the Palestinians from the diaspora, refugees from all over the Arab world, looking for new opportunities of survival.

Life was hard in the Gulf countries, especially for laborers. They worked outdoors at the oil wells and in the cities, in infernal temperatures. They also lived in groups of tens and twenties, huddled together in very small rooms. They managed to send money to their wives at the end of every month to help their families survive, educate their children, and build two or three rooms where they could live.

Those years were better for the intellectuals and office employees who found work in Kuwait and an opportunity to succeed. The best of all those who had studied abroad were here. From a cultural perspective, life among the Palestinians was very lively. But being an outsider was still difficult.

Adnan, with his degree in law, had found a prestigious position at the Ministry of Labor; his job was to write legislation for the workers in Kuwait. He had the protection of a Kuwaiti, which was important since ultimately the Kuwaitis had the power to decide and the last word. Adnan's great charm and charisma were an advantage. He was both known and respected. He would often take me to dinner in the evenings, or to parties and receptions in private homes. The men, who had many more opportunities to move around, would also meet in hotel lobbies, the only public places. The houses that Adnan took me to belonged to the intellectuals: ministers, journalists, and writers. There were English and Americans, but above all Arabs: many Palestinians, Syrians, Iraqis, a few Egyptians, but rarely Kuwaitis, because there was little to exchange with them. There were also a few Iranians. I came to know the cultured class of the Middle East.

This environment fascinated me. I loved the conversations and was impressed by the luxury, the worldliness, the freedom of behavior, and the Western lifestyle. The reception rooms were furnished with low chairs, and always music, suffused with evening light, and hung with heavy drapes to protect from the daytime sun.

Then there was the wall-to-wall carpeting, which was a real novelty. The food, too, was different; it did not require all the work that I was used to. The dishes were simple, but elegant, often cold buffets.

We often went to Ibrahim's brother's house. He was married to a tall, charming, elegant, but somewhat sad young woman who had a degree from the American University in Beirut. Beirut—the very word fascinated me. She often talked to me about Lebanon: It was a democratic country and its capital was a splendid city on the sea with a vibrant intellectual life. There was a lot of freedom there and one could talk openly in cafes, just like in Paris. Ibrahim's brother and wife did not have any children. Their home was relaxing, welcoming—a refined, cultural salon.

I often saw an Iranian there who was handsome, educated, and calm as a prophet. I was fascinated every time I met him. We would speak in English. I knew he was married and that he had three children, but my own adolescent naivety made me think that our relationship, consisting of interesting conversation, was one of love. Naturally I didn't speak to anyone about it, because if Adnan had found out, I would have had to stop seeing him.

Almost all of us were connected with the Ba'ath party. It had just come to power in Syria and in Iraq. There were already Iraqi Ba'ath cells in Kuwait. Party work consisted primarily of propaganda and discussion. It was the intellectual's way of doing politics, somewhat abstract and not focused on concrete political action. I was not used to it and did not like it. Palestine, however, remained at the heart of all the discussions and projects, the bond for every nationalist and revolutionary. It was the central problem for all Arabs.

Adnan, together with others, had founded a left-wing newspaper, which, of course, belonged to the Kuwaitis:

foreigners were not allowed to own anything. It was called *al-Risàla* (the letter). It was one of the first dailies to be published in Kuwait, very liberal and free, with big names writing for it.

Comrades came to party meetings from all over the Middle East. I remember young students and soldiers who came from Iraq, among them Saddam Hussein and others who had participated in various coups d'etat in Iraq. There were also all those Palestinians who later created al-Fatah, one of the main components of the Palestine Liberation Organization (PLO). Many were working in Kuwait at the time, including Yasir Arafat, whom I did not know then, and Abu Lutuf. I remember going to eat at Abu Lutuf's house and meeting there the Palestinian writer Ghassan Kanafani and the genial Iraqi poet Badr Shaker al-Sayab.

The Kuwaitis did not get involved in this intellectual and political activity, because as yet they had no understanding of its implications. The number of Kuwaiti graduates could be counted on the fingers of one hand. The first parliament had been established just shortly before. Intellectual and political life was just beginning.

Contradictions

It was a modern, liberated environment with talk of Marxism, philosophy, music, and politics. We talked of everything, but with all that freedom I still could not smoke a cigarette in front of my brother.

I thought I would be free in Kuwait, but I quickly realized that I was not. It was there that I learned about the duplicity of Arab intellectuals: They called themselves "Marxists" but in practice they were a tangle of contradictions. Publicly they supported women's liberation. They admired strong liberated women, fighters, and they always used them as examples, comparing us with these women, so much so that we wanted to be loved and appreciated in the same way. The comparison was even somewhat humiliating, as if they were saying: "Look, that is a great woman, strong and courageous. She is better than you!" You wanted to have that courage and strength, but inasmuch as you were sister or wife, that freedom was forbidden you. Your freedom had to remain within their control.

Adnan did not like me to smoke. I did not dare ask for a glass of wine and woe betide me if I wore straight skirts. I love tight skirts, but when I sat my legs showed and I had to hide my knees. So arguments broke out between my brother and me. He thought my way of arranging my skirt was false, malicious, and provocative: "You should know that tight skirts rise up your legs. If you don't want to find yourself in that embarrassing position, you should wear other clothes." I answered that I really liked narrow skirts; I did not listen to him and went on wearing them.

I felt oppressed, too, by my brother's friends. They were not really my friends; I had not chosen them. Besides, they were all older than me. They were working; they were married. To them I was just Adnan's little sister—another person's appendage. They all treated me like this, even the women, with whom I had no real friendship, but merely a formal relationship. I began to tire of such a life. I had gone so far to get away from the control of my parents, and I did not want to lose the benefits of that struggle and end up under the control of my brother.

I decided to earn some money so that I could enroll in the university in Syria, and I began insisting that I be allowed to work. My brother succeeded in finding me work as a teacher. It was the only kind of work a woman was permitted in Kuwait. I became a teacher at a middle school called al-Merkab, from the name of the district.

The director called me in for a conference. She too was a Palestinian from Nablus, a tall, strong woman with her hair tied back. She had a determined way and seemed born to be a headmistress. She lived in an apartment in the Teacher's Residence with an elderly mother and a sister who taught physical education in the same school. The school was her whole world.

She looked at me and laughed at my braids, my low shoes, and my young girl's appearance: "You are a teacher now and when the inspector comes from the Ministry of Public Education, he must be able to distinguish the teacher from the student. You must change your appearance. Cut your hair, put on some make-up and high heels. You need to look more feminine and more grown-up." I was amused and disturbed by her advice. I decided to follow it after my first class. My pupils were intimidating and looked me up and down. It was obvious that I was—or at least looked—younger than they.

I was to teach literature to the second and third middle school grades, and many of the girls were in fact older than me. Some of them had repeated the same class as many as four times. They came to school because it was their only chance to get out of the house. They wore heavy make-up and showed off their entire wardrobes. They went to school as if they were going to a picnic or a beauty salon.

It was difficult to work with them and being a foreigner made matters worse. You are there to carry away a little of their wealth, to be paid by them at the end of the month. And so they regard you and treat you as their servant.

It was always obvious with the Kuwaitis that they were the bosses. They behaved with arrogance and exhibited an air of superiority. They were diffident; perhaps they had an inferiority complex in front of us Palestinians who were, after all, building their country. We are a very proud, strong people, difficult to buy or subdue. I was not surprised at the Palestinian diaspora from Kuwait during the Gulf War. It could have been predicted.

The janitorial work at the school was reserved for the Kuwaitis. They were fat women always to be found sitting on the ground, gossiping and drinking tea. Their salary was four times a teacher's salary, and they had chauffeur-driven Mercedes waiting for them outside the school. To be a janitor was a sign of great emancipation for them, a kind of luxury. They were not working out of necessity, but just to have something to do.

The Kuwaitis were spoiled by free education and health care. They were even able to go abroad for their health. The few who wanted to study at the university were given generous scholarships. There was no reason for them to work or make an effort. And they were so stingy that they reacted nervously when anyone greeted them; they were afraid you were going to ask for something. Fortunately my contact with them was very limited. The Kuwaitis themselves were, after all, a minority in the middle of that hodgepodge of population that made up Kuwait.

The rule was that unmarried teachers must live in the Teacher's Residence. And so I also moved in to the big house, where I shared a room with another young woman from Nablus. Every two rooms shared a bathroom. On the ground floor was a large kitchen with many tables where you could cook and eat in company. Next to it was a living room with a television.

The building was constructed in such a way that no one could see us from the outside: it was surrounded by a small garden and then a cement wall, with cracks through which you could scarcely put a finger. From there you could spy on what was going on outside without ever being seen. A bit like a prison!

Kuwaiti society was very closed and women were required to hide behind walls or beneath the *abbaya*. This black cloak of light material goes over a woman's head and she holds it closed under her chin. It hangs down to the feet; only her face remains uncovered. Some Kuwaiti women even covered their face with a very beautiful mask, which only left the eyes uncovered. There was something fascinating about those big black eyes, which you could glimpse under the cloak.

Putting on the *abbaya* before going out was a tradition, a social obligation, a law that no woman could avoid, not even a foreigner. In the beginning it was difficult for me to get used to it, but after a while I found that it was a very comfortable garment. It protected you from the sand carried by the winds, which caused eye diseases, and it helped me avoid getting scorched when I got into a car that had been boiling in the sun. The garment was full and the air could circulate within it. Even men, in fact, wore full white garments without belts. It was a way of adapting to the climate before it became a religious custom.

It was also convenient in that it provided protection from the male gaze. Your body became invisible, only an indistinct shape beneath that cloak. In it, I never felt that someone was looking at my body or my clothes. You could wear a Chanel suit or a nightshirt underneath and no one would know the difference. The *abbaya* is a garment that gives one great freedom, even if it unquestionably erases a woman's identity.

The teachers living at the Residence came from all over the Arab world, but were predominantly Palestinian and Egyptian. It was there that I became aware of the cultural differences among the Arab countries. I was pleased about the presence of Egyptians because I liked Nasser a lot and the millennial Egypt, the Egypt of writers, films, and songs. There were many Egyptian graduates. But they were not as serious and involved as I had expected; nor were they interested in politics and culture.

My friend Nadira was typical. She had imagination— she was always laughing and telling stories and she was carefree and generous. She had a beautiful voice and used to walk through the corridors singing and trying out dance steps. It was fun to go shopping with her because she knew no limits: like everyone, she was crazy about textiles, shoes, and gold, but she also liked domestic appliances. She would buy refrigerators, washing machines, and things for the house. When she went back to Egypt at the end of each year, she would always leave with enormous suitcases and mail big packages.

Egypt had a socialist system so the importing of consumer goods was the exclusive privilege of those who worked abroad. The Egyptian women took maximum advantage of this right of theirs, and upon their return to Egypt they sold most of what they had bought. This made it possible for them to put aside clothes and furniture for a house that might become an incentive for an eventual suitor, and still have money for purchases the following year.

The young women from Syria were different. They were more autonomous in their way of thinking. They wanted to buy a house and secure assets that would ensure their future; they wanted an income, which would give them protection. Syria was a freer, richer, and more developed country. This, combined with other things, made it easier for women to think about their lives independently from men. Moreover, Syrians had a well-deserved reputation of being smart business people, paying attention to what was solid.

I was a little envious of them, but I also thought I was better than my Syrian companions. We Palestinians, after all, were very diverse. We worked in order to help our families and not be a burden to them. The tragedy that had united us was still very recent and all of us, men and women, felt responsible for each other. Apart from Nadira, the Egyptian, my dearest friends were all Palestinian.

Fathia was one of my roommates. She belonged to a middle-class family from Gaza and had studied in Cairo. She knew some important people and felt somewhat superior because of her social class. However her problems with her family made her critical and angry at life and brought her closer to my way of thinking. We stayed in touch even after we had left Kuwait and she came to see me in Vienna.

There was also Alia, a young woman from Nablus, a little older than me, who had been a school friend. She was one of the few young women in Kuwait with whom I could talk politics. She was a communist and her father was someone important in the Jordanian army; he had participated in a coup d'etat and been sent away to a foreign country. She, too, enrolled in the university in Damascus, so we went to Syria together to sit for the exams. In the end she married a doctor and went to live in the United States.

With Warda, a Syrian Palestinian, I carried on an intense dialogue. We talked about life, women, and our futures. We both wanted affection, security, and a family, but she was more traditional. I continued to long for new experiences. She married an engineer who was working in Kuwait. We continued to see each other—I would go to their house on Fridays—but marriage changed her and I felt somewhat rejected.

There were not only fresh and hopeful young women at the Residence, but also a group of older teachers in their 30s and 40s. They were a disturbing presence because they marked the limits of what I could achieve.

They liked me and made a fuss over me because I was the youngest. They would help me when it was my turn to wash dishes or cook; they would clean my room and wash my clothes. Sometimes they got together in a little group for waxing and they would invite me to join in this custom. They would prepare the wax themselves with sugar and lemon, and then pluck my hairs, while I stretched out and read a book.

When I stopped to consider their lives, though, I became very upset to think of the years they had spent far from their own countries, with no opportunity of meeting anyone. Time had passed as they grew old and remained spinsters. Some had been in love once, but because they needed to work they had had to postpone their wedding until finally the lover had left.

Their existence was monotonous. They would come home from school, cook, eat, and take a rest. Afternoons and evenings were spent in front of the television watching stupid films, telling vulgar jokes, and playing cards. I grew to hate card games at the Residence, and at friends' houses too. Women played cards to pass the useless time they spent waiting for the men to come home from their interminable parties.

At other times they stretched out on the sofas in the living room and talked for hours about men and sex. It was the same at my friend Lubna's house, which I had been visiting since I first arrived in Kuwait. I did not want to get involved in these conversations. That environment of women only, where the other half of the world was missing, where love between man and woman was forbidden, created a kind of morbidity that reminded me of the women's college in Ramallah. A love between women, even fantasized, became a fascinating tale for everyone. I gradually came to detest that atmosphere.

They loved the songs of Farid al-Atrash and Abd el-Halim about impossible love affairs. But most of all they loved the Egyptian Umm Kulthum, the most famous female singer in the Arab world.

Umm Kulthum was and still is today—despite her death—a kind of drug for the entire Arab population. It is even said that during a crisis in Egypt, Nasser asked her to write a new song and that the Egyptian army suffered a surprise attack during the Six-Day War because all the soldiers were listening to Umm Kulthum. Many were ready to spend their entire savings on going to one of her concerts.

She was a big woman with a lovely face. She always held a handkerchief in her hand when she was singing. Her songs were very long: about fate, solitude, and lost loves. Some lyrics were the poetry of Nizar Qabbani or of the fabulous Tunisian poet, Abul-Qasim al-Shabi.

When one of her concerts was announced on the radio, my companions would throw a party. They would start preparing two days before. They got together and cooked all sorts of good things, repeating verses from her songs, joking among themselves and becoming very rowdy. They felt united. Then came the concert and melancholy prevailed. Each one cried for her lost opportunities, her ruined life, and her fear of loneliness. Each one traced her own story in the lines of the songs. I didn't want to get involved in that atmosphere of sadness and regret. I would say goodbye and run to my room where I would remain alone, reading and studying. Someone would eventually come looking for me. They thought I was crazy.

My favorite singer was Fairouz. She was not very well known, especially by the Egyptians, but she was dearly loved by us Palestinians and by the Lebanese. She herself is Lebanese and is still writing and singing, and today rivals Umm Kulthum throughout the whole Arab world.

Fairouz belonged to the counterculture. Short songs, a strong voice, and a style that was a marvelous mix of East and West. She sang about the little and big things in life, she sang about flowers, birds, the stairs in her house when she was little, and about childhood and old age, love, nostalgia, and returning. All the things whose importance and beauty you don't recognize until you have lost them.

Even today when I listen to her, she can stir in me the same emotion as when I was young. "*Sanàrgia yau-man ila hayyina*" (One day we shall return to our neighborhood...) tears me apart and overwhelms me with emotion. I have always had immense admiration for this great person who is a poet, a philosopher. When I was a patient in the hospital in Houston, a famous Lebanese doctor told me that I reminded him of Fairouz: I considered that a huge compliment.

My Opportunity for Independence

I had never had any money except when I was invited by relatives for Eid al-Kabir (the feast of sacrifice) or to celebrate the end of Ramadan. These were the only occasions I was given money, and I managed to make it last the whole year.

Economic independence was a marvelous challenge for me. The stipend at the end of the month made me drunk with joy—it gave me a feeling of freedom, independence, and strength. The money I earned enabled me that year, 1960, to enroll in the university in Damascus.

I had always meant to enroll in the Faculty of Science, but I would have had to attend class; that would have meant that I could no longer teach and be economically independent. Instead I chose philosophy, the most demanding of the humanities. I had always liked philosophy. I chose Syria because the Ba'ath party was in power there and because it was a developed country. The people of Damascus were very open in attitude; life there was lively, with theaters, nightclubs, and restaurants. The university followed the same system as the Sorbonne in Paris and there was a strong and active student organization. It was possible to participate in politics, which interested me.

I taught all year in Kuwait and went to Damascus in the summer to take exams. Alia had given me the address of a Syrian friend of hers who attended the university and who could help me in my long-distance studies. Nawal sent me the notes, obtained the books for me and kept me abreast of everything. We exchanged letters for a whole year without seeing each other. It was a big surprise when I met her for the first time at the airport. She was elegantly dressed in a long robe, with her hair covered. She was tiny with a gracious face and timid smile. I stayed at the student residence in Damascus and when there was no room I went to a boarding house. I studied with Nawal.

When I finished my exams, I left for Nablus. I arrived, exhausted from the year of grueling hard work. As usual I had a fever and I spent my first days at home sick. Then I renewed my studies in preparation for the fall exams. When I left again, it was first to Damascus and then back to work in Kuwait. It was not the university life of my dreams.

It was grueling, but still my independence made me very happy. Had I stayed at Nablus, the best I could have done would be to find a teaching position in some little village. I would have had to go back and forth from my home, which my father would not have permitted.

Instead, in Kuwait, I had more freedom; I could live as I wished. Moreover I did not have to ask my family for a penny for the university: I paid my own keep, bought my own books, and paid for my travels and my two months' stay in Damascus.

I discovered how nice it was not to depend on my father, my brother, or anyone else. A woman's freedom begins with her economic independence. Not only did I not have to ask anyone for money, but I could even buy my mother and sisters presents, and have enough left over to give my father something for the house and the orchard. Every year I gave my mother a big present. The first was a washing machine. That was my revenge for all the years of being asked to help wash the clothes. At first my mother did not want to believe that it would wash better than by hand, but then I proved it and she realized how convenient it was. She was very happy and almost ready to forgive me for all the times that I had not helped. I believe "Salwa's washing machine" lasted until a short time ago. My sisters adored and admired me. My return home was a joy. They received me like a queen and I felt spoiled and fussed over.

Teaching also gave me great satisfaction, despite my difficulties with the young Kuwaiti women who were often rebellious and interested in humiliating the teacher and making her look ridiculous. Sometimes some of the teachers, especially the Egyptians, left their classrooms in tears. Rebellion was risky.

I, on the other hand, had learned how to treat these difficult young women. I came to an arrangement with the smartest of them, those with the strongest personalities, and made them responsible. I never needed to call the director to resolve a problem.

I stressed the importance of reading. I wanted to teach these young women to become familiar with books. I managed to take them to the library for an hour. They had never read a book in their lives that wasn't a textbook, and now they could request the loan of books and reviews; they could study arguments in depth.

One day one of my pupils who was very enthusiastic

about my methods gave me a record player (the students were permitted to have them). I put the record player in the library, made them listen to Fairouz at low volume, in the background. At first they didn't like her, but slowly they began to appreciate her. They even listened to classical music for the first time.

I would urge them to look around, and sometimes even made them do it. Ever since I was a child, I had known that it was important to have someone to help you, someone who would almost force you to discover things, because you cannot always wait for the right occasion. My pupils came to understand and remained fond of me even after they left school. Anyone who could continued to study literature and many of them, to my great surprise, had called their children Yara or Rima—the short, modern names of the women in Fairouz's songs.

I managed to introduce new initiatives into the school. I created a school radio-show. Using a microphone and loudspeakers, we transmitted a program similar to the one on the radio. A half-hour, with twenty minutes of poetry, Arab sayings, and political and cultural information. On certain important occasions, such as historical Arab anniversaries, we provided more in-depth information. I often spoke about Palestine, explaining its history, talking about the Balfour declaration and the struggles during the 1930s and the disaster of 1948. We included nationalist music and songs, and we also told jokes. Finally, while the pupils filed to their classes, we transmitted the "March over the River Kwai." We tried to make the program varied, fast, and amusing. Something both useful and different.

And, in fact, the girls followed it with interest. Some of them helped prepare the daily programs. The idea was a success. Even the teachers liked it and it was the envy of the neighboring boys' school.

Logic and the Heart

But life in the middle of a desert did not and could not satisfy me. I looked at the men and women around me. They had come to Kuwait with the intention of spending only a few years there, but they could not manage to leave. Kuwait had become a habit that was difficult to break. Because of responsibility to others and to our country, because of the ease of earning a living, because of a lack of other possibilities, no one could make up their mind to leave. They lived in this isolated desert, far from home, full of nostalgia, dissatisfied.

I, too, began to feel a victim of the situation. I grew afraid of the prospect of being stuck in that oppressive desert, not able to break away.

I had grown up and I wanted a private life of my own. I wanted to marry, start a family, have children, and enable them to do what I had not been able to do. Solitude had never appealed to me and I had never been a dedicated enough feminist to think of living alone. I wanted to have a family I could raise with affection and responsibility.

And so I fell in love. He was a Palestinian, a very gentle, helpful young man who showed his feelings with great tenderness. He was a simple person, overpowered by his important brother's personality. I enjoyed his company, but I didn't want to encourage the relationship. To become engaged to him would mean remaining in Kuwait, and that I did not want to do.

Kuwait had nothing more to offer me. Even my relationship with Adnan had deteriorated. He controlled me and looked on me as his property. It was a different sort of control than that of my parents. He paid me many compliments and told me that no man deserved me, but using this as an excuse he did not allow me to have relationships with anyone. When I talked to him about my plans he laughed in my face and told me that it was wrong for me to tie myself to a man who could become a disaster. I answered that I wanted to find that out for myself.

After a great deal of effort, a Kuwaiti deputy of the Ba'ath party, our only representative, managed to get elected to parliament. He always came to our meetings and listened to our conversations about freedom and unity in the Arab world. He was fascinated by our lifestyle and fell in love with me. The poor fellow dared to ask for my hand in marriage from my brother, which he should never have done. Adnan lost his head and threw him out of the house. He broke off all political and friendly contact with the man simply because he had had "the courage to think he was on my level."

After that, Adnan's friends were forbidden territory. After all the talk that had gone on about me, no one dared to come near me. I could not put up with my brother always making decisions for me any longer.

After sitting for the exams in Damascus in the summer of 1964, I went home to Nablus as usual. I racked my brains to find a way to get out of the life in Kuwait. I knew that it was virtually impossible for a young woman to make a life for herself alone. I did not want to give up the possibility of having a family, nor did I want to marry someone unknown, chosen by my family, as tradition demanded.

During the holiday period in Nablus there were often visits from the so-called *khuttab* who came to ask for my hand in marriage. The mother and sisters would call on us, and sometimes the interested man to whom they had pointed me out on the street or somewhere. They would come with information about themselves and their son.

It was the custom for the young woman to bring in tea or coffee as an excuse to show herself. Instead I would escape by the back door, so they could not find me. I hated the *khuttab*—they frightened and horrified me, examining me from head to toe and looking at me like a piece of merchandise. I felt stripped by their eyes. I rejected the idea and could not imagine marrying a man who came to show me his graduation certificate and his bank account.

My flights would put my parents in an embarrassing situation and for that I was sorry. I was becoming a problem for my family: everyone worried about my future, including me. I refused this type of arranged marriage but I did not have the courage to develop a personal relationship of my own. The thought of choosing a husband by myself scared me. It meant breaking completely with tradition, which was a very serious thing for the honor of my father and unacceptable at any social level.

The house was tranquil that summer. All my sisters were there because they had not yet started university. My parents were serene, more relaxed than they used to be.

Also they thought I was stupid. It made me suspicious any time they whispered or exchanged looks. I tried to guess what was going on, and would send my sisters at five o'clock in the morning to listen behind the door, when they were chatting after prayers.

They kept talking about a family with whom they were friendly. My mother liked this family a lot. They were from Haifa, and the father had worked on the railroad during the time of the British. They, too, had been forced to leave their home, their work, and their land in 1948. Fortunately, like us, they had relatives in the country near Nablus and took refuge with them. The father had succeeded in finding work in Saudi Arabia, which had made it possible for them to put money aside and begin to build a big new house in Jordan.

I understood that they intended for me to get to know the son. He was studying medicine in Vienna and was very intelligent. But they pretended there was nothing going on. It amused me and seemed a little different from the other times: it was well camouflaged by an air of friendship, as though they were leaving it to us young folk. I was not sure of their plans.

One day I was told that this entire family would be coming to see us: mother, father, sisters and brothers, six or seven people, an army! Everyone at home continued to pretend that it was all normal, an innocent visit. I decided to play along, but meanwhile my curiosity grew.

The day came and I got ready. The children's shrieks in the street announced the arrival of our guests. I hid behind the curtains on the veranda and watched them enter. There was a tall, large young man... perhaps it was he. I didn't like him. Then another came in, thin, with a light blue suit, a marvelous delicate face with joining eyebrows. He looked like Omar Sharif. Was he the young man of whom I had heard so much talk? My heart was beating and I trembled with emotion.

We all went into the living room and started a conversation. They presented Muhammad to me. He was young, barely a year older than me. Educated, refined, cultured. He did not look at me—not at my legs, my breasts, my teeth, but instead spoke of his experiences in Vienna and his life there. He talked about serious things, about politics. He had a beautiful voice. And he did not look me over; I did not feel humiliated and measured like a piece of merchandise as with the other *khuttab*.

He made a deep impression on me. I had always thought that love at first sight was stupid, the stuff of romances, but this time it was happening to me. And the thought that he, handsome and with the means to live well, could have young European women, blond bright-eyed Viennese, and yet came looking for a Palestinian life partner—that was something marvelous and deserving of respect. Generally anyone who went to study in another country ended up marrying a young woman from there. Instead, Muhammad wanted to do the opposite, and this filled me with admiration.

If I really wanted to get married without breaking with tradition, then this was the right person. He suited both my heart and my logic. Since I was a fairly practical person, I also thought that this encounter would offer me a new experience, a chance to know Europe, the mother of civilization, the most beautiful place in the world. Vienna was famous at the time. My favorite professor at the university in Damascus had graduated in Vienna. And the old singer, Asmahan, used to sing a song with the words *"la-yali al-ouns fi Vienna..."* (nights of joy in Vienna).

Moreover it seemed easier and better to begin the adventure with a man of the same age in a distant place, where together we would be able to carry out all our plans. We could study in Europe and then return home. I wanted to teach in the university and produce cultural programs on television.

Inside, I rejoiced at my marvelous luck: I thought that I had found everything: a man whom I liked and Vienna, where I could continue my studies. It was the solution to all my problems. I felt at ease because I could finish my studies before marrying, and two years would give me time to know him better. If we did not get along, we could forget the idea.

The visits were repeated and thanks to the good sense of our parents, Muhammad and I were given a chance to talk and get to know each other a little. The negotiations between our families progressed and the official engagement took place prior to my departure for Kuwait.

At this point I broke another rule. Traditionally the husband was supposed to pay his fiancée's family a certain sum, a kind of dowry, which would be used to prepare for marriage, clothes, and a house. It was a useful custom and served a social function, especially for families with a lot of daughters, since they were obliged to prepare them all for marriage. This sum was given in two installments: the *muqaddam* before the wedding and the *mu'akhkhar* after.

I refused it. I told my father: "Papa, I have my own money. I am not a burden on you so I don't want the money from Muhammad's family. I don't want him to be able to say to me one day, if we quarrel, 'I paid so much for you.'" Naturally my father flew into a rage: According to him, not accepting the dowry meant that I had no value and that he was giving his daughter away. I explained that it wasn't that way for me, nor for Muhammad. Moreover, I was leaving for Europe and would not need to get a house ready. I really did not want the money; I wanted to rely solely on my own resources. The discussion went on for days, but in the end I convinced him—I made it a condition for my marriage.

The day came for our official engagement. The marriage contract was quickly settled, even though we would not be married for two years. This was done sometimes to protect the woman in case something unfortunate should happen during the engagement period, a pregnancy for example. Every problem would be taken care of with a contract.

There was a real engagement party. I was the first person in the family to get engaged and it was a very important occasion for my father. He really loved parties and so he made a big thing of it. He invited dozens of people; and there were a lot of waiters to serve coffee and drinks to the guests. The guests were all men who came from Nablus and from the nearby villages, bringing gifts of sacks of rice, pigs, coffee, sugar, and other useful things in enormous quantities. They all wanted to shake hands with the father of the groom and the father of the bride. It was primarily a party for my father and his friends. Muhammad and I did not seem to enter into the picture. Muhammad got tired of all that ceremony early and did not hesitate to leave a friend in his place; I stayed far away in another room, with the women and the men of my family. When the imam arrived to make the contract, they called me to give my formal consent. Naturally I answered yes, and that was my only participation in my engagement party. I found it all somewhat ridiculous but I did not say a word, not wanting to spoil my father's joy.

The festivities over, we remained in Nablus another ten days or so, then we each went our own way. I took the exams in Damascus and returned to Kuwait.

Matrimony

There was usually a delegation to meet me when I arrived at the airport, but this time no one was there—only a car and chauffeur to take me directly to the Residence. I had not asked Adnan's opinion about my engagement to Muhammad. I had made my own decision and for him this was the worst thing in the world.

Even though our relationship became strained as a result, it did not matter to me because I was convinced that I had made the right decision. True, it was a bit of a shock for all my friends—Salwa getting married according to tradition. They were curious and wondered what sort of a young man could break down my resistance.

I was very much in love and distance only increased this feeling. Perhaps it even made me idealize the man I was to marry. We exchanged letters for two years. My mood depended on the arrival of letters from Vienna.

I loved to write and even sent Muhammad two letters every week, very long letters of ten or twenty pages. I described the social, political, and intimate details of my daily life; I told him everything that happened around me. He answered me in letters of three or four pages at most, very controlled, but I could tell there was a lot of affection. He told me about Vienna, said that life there wasn't great, and that in his opinion there were not many interesting things to relate, but that it would be better when we were together. He made no promises and his tone was always very serious.

This seemed strange because, for me, Vienna seemed the center of the world and I could not wait to get there. On the other hand his way of being so serious and reserved made me curious and intrigued me all the more. His apparent distance increased my desire to win him over.

For two years the idea of marriage and life in Europe occupied all my thoughts. I made plans, imagining the future. I had great confidence in my ability and felt strong enough to overcome any difficulty. I was proud of myself because I was leaving Kuwait. And also I was very much in love—perhaps with an idea of my own, perhaps I was in love with love, but certainly I was determined to follow the road I had chosen to its end.

My last year of teaching in Kuwait was great and very exciting. I had so many things to do in preparation for my departure. I made purchases, thinking that, at least for a few years, I would not be able to buy anything, because we would be living in Vienna as students. I bought some wool sweaters, knowing that it was very cold there.

My friends gave many farewell parties for me. Some of them envied me and said: "Lucky you. You're terrific! Vienna is the only place for which to leave Kuwait." Others were envious of the love I had found. They were emotional parties with tears and many demonstrations of affection. Even the school director was very warm toward me, despite my not having been a docile participant.

I realized that I had spent six of the most fundamental years of my life in Kuwait. I had grown up there and become independent, made many important connections. That experience had given me the strength to create my own life as I had always imagined.

I left Kuwait, and before going to Nablus I returned as usual to Damascus. I knew that I would not be able to finish my exams, but I did all that I could. I would sit for the remaining few after my marriage. I remember going out on one of my last evenings in Damascus with my friends, both men and women. We saw Lorca's *Nights of Blood* and afterward went out to an elegant place. Those were happy, serene days.

When I got back to Nablus, I found everything upside down and everyone in a fever of preparation. Muhammad arrived a few days later. We had fixed our wedding day to coincide with the end of the academic year. At home there were my parents, the youngest girls Badia and Nadia, Rima, Iqbal, and Ihsan. Feryal was not able to come because of his university studies and Asnan and Issam were in Kuwait because their vacation period had already ended.

My wedding took place some twenty days later, on September 10, 1966. I had my hair done at the hairdresser's. Then they put on my makeup at home. I wore an embroidered, very elegant gown of white silk, long with a low neckline and an extremely long white veil, which Nadia and Badia held.

They moved the last of the furniture; everything had been turned upside down to make room for the guests. Right up to the last moment I begged them not to put up a platform for the armchairs of the married couple, as tradition had it. "We'll sit in the chairs, but I can't agree to stay there on the platform, like statues, immobile!" It was bad enough to have to sit still in front of all those people and let myself be looked at while they all had fun. I managed to get my way. It was slightly less embarrassing, but just the same I was very tense.

Finally, the celebration began. The house filled with women: cousins, aunts, my mother's friends, neighbors. There were only three or four of my own friends. The music started and they began to sing and clap their hands. They danced in front of me, laughing and talking loudly, making their *zagharit*. They sent laughter to me. It was everyone else's celebration rather than mine. It was a celebration for my mother and for all the women; it was they who were having a good time. I would have preferred to be laughing myself and talking among my friends—that way it would have been more of a celebration for me.

After the women's celebration, the groom came with all his family. I had spoken with Muhammad on the phone that morning and knew that he too was bothered by all the fuss.

It is the custom for the groom on his wedding day to give his bride necklaces, bracelets, and gold earrings according to his economic means. The bride then had to put on the jewelry. The important thing was for everyone to see it; it is the magical moment of the whole celebration. Everyone was looking at me, trying to guess the value of the objects I had been given, so they could talk about it.

I remember that the ceremony went on too long; I felt really uncomfortable and could not wait for it to be over. I was deprived of will power, I felt like a walk-on rather than the star, an object in others' hands. Muhammad had actually put on a pair of dark glasses in order not to see people, to remove himself, as it were, from them. He kept his glasses on the whole time. The day really dragged. We had to have patience—we had to please our parents. After all it was their celebration—we would be leaving, and they would be left with all this.

With the festivities over, the moment came to leave for Muhammad's house. From then on I belonged to him—I had become a member of another family. For the first time, I felt something break inside me. My mother was crying, my sisters were crying as if we were saying goodbye. I will never forget the face of my father, who was trying to hide his feelings. I too was crying, but I was happy to go with Muhammad.

The hardest thing to overcome was the idea that I had to spend that night in his family's house. We didn't have a house of our own because we were leaving for Vienna and it was not possible to spend the night in a hotel. However we had agreed to go through with this comedy to the end, when we would be able to be together on our own terms.

Rooms had been made ready for us at Muhammad's house, a kind of mini-apartment just for us. It was already difficult for me to get used to the idea of sleeping with a man and I would have preferred a more private, more intimate setting. But we were happy, excited, in seventh heaven: it was the first time we had been alone together in two years.

That evening friends and relatives came to call under the windows and knock at the doors to offer us stuffed chicken, sweets, and desserts. That was the custom.

But the worst was to follow when members of his family would come the next day to inspect the sheets. According to Palestinian tradition, it is important to consummate the marriage physically, since that means that all is well with both husband and wife, that a prosperous life can begin, and honor is redeemed.

Fortunately they were very sensitive: I believe that they went to inspect the sheets at a time when I was not there, or they asked Muhammad something. They spared me this big humiliation, partly because they knew me and knew that I only went along with tradition up to a certain point, and partly because Muhammad, too, objected to this ritual. His father had been in Saudi Arabia while he was growing up. He had always gone to boarding schools and had lived in Europe, so he did not feel all these obligations to his family and to tradition. He was a reserved person, not liking to be put on show, and very protective of his intimacy.

That afternoon a huge number of guests came for a special meal to congratulate us and wish us well, and I had to stand there and smile and join in the festivities. What was most moving was to greet my parents as if they were guests. That was very hard to get used to.

I had to leave for Damascus a few days later in order to take the exams for which I had not prepared, but which I had to take if I were not to lose the year. I would have liked for Muhammad to go with me but that was not possible. He had been politically active in Vienna and had had problems with the Syrian embassy: he preferred to remain at home in order to avoid trouble.

A few days after I returned from Damascus, we left for Vienna. I could finally put an end to the whole comedy. We left from the airport between Jerusalem and Ramallah—these days it is occupied by the Israelis. I remember that lots of people came to see us off.

I was with Muhammad, our life together was beginning, the two of us alone. I was very moved and excited, as at the beginning of a new adventure. I was full of dreams, plans, and fantasies.

FOUR

Vienna
1966–1970

Disillusionment with the West

I was about to live the dream that had been with me for two years. I would be having "nights of joy in Vienna"— I would go to the Opera and to the Philharmonic to hear Beethoven and Mozart; I would specialize in child psychology, my latest desire; I would begin my married life. I was full of enthusiasm. I thought I had the world in my hands and that there would be no obstacles.

My husband, on the other hand, was somewhat morose; certainly his thoughts were different from mine, and I found this hard to understand. I did not yet know him well enough.

We arrived in Vienna at sunset. Three of Muhammad's friends were waiting for us and one of them had a bunch of flowers for me. I was moved because it was the first time that I had received a gift like that. I considered it a Western refinement, an elegant gesture learned in Vienna.

We drove through a dark and almost deserted city, full of enormous, dark buildings. As they said, "Look on the right... look on the left," I caught glimpses of splendid angles, but what struck me most were the huge, black ancient buildings. The houses and the streets were run-down and dilapidated. My mouth dropped open. The houses in our country were made of shining white stone. I knew that Vienna was different, that it had an ancient history, but I had imagined Europe as a shining, new place, full of modernity, magic, and novelty. I never tired of gazing and was constantly amazed.

Our friends took us to a hotel in the center of the city. It was ancient and different from any hotel I had ever seen. We were given a spacious room with wooden floors, antique furniture, and a frescoed ceiling.

I was very impressed and excited, especially when we ended the evening by going to the Wiener Wald, a typically Viennese restaurant in Grinzing, an area in the hills just outside of Vienna. I had imagined an elegant, modern place full of lights. Instead it was very ordinary with dark wood and large tables of solid walnut. The waitresses were fat and hurried, and wore traditional Viennese dresses. It was part of a chain of restaurants scattered all over Austria, with a set menu: roast chicken, fried potatoes, and beet and cucumber salad with a lot of dressing. We were used to eating chicken at home so this was nothing new. Many customers were drunk, shouting and singing cheerfully. It was the place in Asmahan's song: this was the joy of Vienna. But I did not feel at ease, nor was I very happy. I was incapable of getting drunk, and I could not forget myself. It seemed a strange way to have fun. It was not the first time that I had seen people drinking—even in Kuwait some people drank, but they did not let themselves go with such enjoyment.

We were quiet and serious, especially because I was there. My arrival in Vienna had caused a great stir; it was the first time that a student had had the courage to marry a woman from his own country and bring her to live in such a different world where young Arab women were scarcely ever seen. There was admiration—but also curiosity to see the outcome. They did not think it was suitable for an Arab woman to come to Europe. They believed it would be too difficult for her to adapt to a new and different world.

Young Palestinian Arabs have never been able to resolve their contradictions and their dual inclinations. They act like chickens with European women and like fathers and masters with women from their own country. With European women they are permissive, accepting everything and even openly admiring their freedom; whereas they expect women from their own country to follow the traditions "because it is necessary to remain faithful to one's cultural identity." This reasoning has always offended me. I consider it a lack of maturity and a logic that is behind the times.

All evening we talked of politics, of news from home and of our Palestine. The others talked about people whom I had not yet met. I was curious. There was so much to discover and learn.

Almost immediately I grew fond of a café called Aida. It was one of a chain of cafes situated throughout the city. These were not traditional Viennese cafés, but more modern, with glass windows to sit beside and look out. They served only desserts, Viennese specialties, and it was there that I first tasted *apfel strudel* and a kind of brioche filled with ricotta. Those are the only things that I really miss from Vienna.

For a while I was a tourist. There were monuments, buildings, squares, gardens, and flowers everywhere—

splendid sights. I was ecstatic, gazing around, asking questions and making comments like a stupid child.

Before long, to my great pleasure we went to the cinema; I had not set foot in a cinema since the early days in Nablus when it was an adventure. There were no movie theaters in Kuwait and I never had the time in Damascus.

Muhammad had lived with other students before his marriage and had not managed to find a place for the two of us. People did not want to rent to foreigners and when there was something available, it was so expensive that three or four people would have to live there. The alternative was to live on the outskirts, far from the center. But I wanted to live in the center so that I could go out alone, explore the city, and walk to the university.

We searched for a long time and even our friends went out of their way to help us. Finally, after experiencing a lot of distrust, we succeeded in meeting a certain Mr. Sonntag. He seemed almost surprised to meet me. I was a human being. The discovery seemed to reassure him: he said that I seemed a respectable young woman and that he would rent us the rooms, which he praised to the skies.

They were situated in Van Swietengasse, a little street in the center, at right angles to Wahringerstrasse, near the hospital and the university. We entered a small old building through a little entrance that was carved like the bigger entrances. We found ourselves on a dark staircase, because the landlord was unwilling to use the electricity.

Our apartment was on a first floor landing that was even darker than the staircase. Mr. Sonntag opened the door. The hallway was a small windowless room without heat, with two chairs and a table. It led into a larger room with a big window and a large, high double bed, a kind of wardrobe, and an old gas stove. Two threadbare curtains hid the cooking alcove and the door to a small bathroom.

My head was spinning and my heart was breaking in pieces. This was my first house. It was to have been my dream house in Europe and instead... I was disappointed and squeezed my eyes so as not to cry in front of my husband and his friends. They were saying that it was a unique opportunity, not to be lost, and that better places than this would be difficult to find. I nodded my head in acceptance since my voice choked in my throat.

I felt wounded, excluded, marginalized. The reality of racism was new to me; it was the first time I had to come to grips with it. I had put up with the arrogance of the Kuwaitis, who felt they were the masters of the world. But their racism was ignorance, an inferiority complex in the face of the Palestinians.

This Viennese racism was different, systematic; if you were a foreigner they would not rent to you and treated you like a worm because you did not deserve anything better. And it could not be said that the Europeans were ignorant. Why then were they racists? And why with us? I felt I was equal to the Austrians. We had a great tradition, a great civilization, a great history of which we were very proud. In what way could they feel superior, better than us? Furious, I wondered why this was the culture that I had come to discover. I wanted to discuss it with them, but unfortunately I had not yet learned German.

Despite this not very positive beginning, I did not lose heart. I wanted to learn German quickly and set to work at once. Muhammad and his friends gave me books and, thanks to them, I began to study, enrolling in a German course at the university.

I could walk there because it was close to our house. There were students from all over Europe. They knew a little more German than I, but I studied hard and soon caught up with them.

For a long time my fellow students and teachers treated me as though I was a Martian. They knew I was Palestinian, so they asked me: "Exactly what is a *Palestinian?*" I answered "an Arab," but that prompted smiles and irony. "Then where did you learn to dress like a civilized person? How do you like walking in shoes? When did you wear shoes for the first time? Is it easier to go barefoot or with shoes?" Offended and irritated, I answered in English or in my shaky German. I tried to explain that their ideas were ridiculous, that I had not learned to put shoes on in Vienna, but had always worn them, and the same with my clothes. But they insisted. They considered Arabs to be underdeveloped, primitive, and backward. In addition, I was a woman and that sparked other questions: "Where is your veil? Aren't you afraid to go out in the street?" In their minds, Arab women were those black, shrouded creatures, barefoot, stained, without personality. They saw that I was annoyed. Perhaps they were afraid that I had stolen their way of being.

I decided to bring my wedding photo to school, to show where I came from. The album passed from hand to hand through the whole class. My companions were amazed and looked and looked at the photos. I was wearing a white wedding dress with a long veil, and they saw all those elegant people around me. Only princesses and actresses got married in such style in the Vienna of those days. They themselves got married in jeans, or short pants, or in a dress straight from the factory, not in a garment hand-sewn by a dressmaker. A wedding like mine was something for the newspapers, a big worldly event. They looked at me astounded and compared me with the photographs, because they could not come to terms with the idea. I had greatly confused them. They could not imagine that such a wedding and ceremony could be for an Arab woman.

They began to ask: "But are you sure you are Arab? Did you really live in Arab countries?" Perhaps that was the cruelest aspect of their attitude. "Absolutely, I am sure of it," I answered. "I am Arab, and I am not a princess—nor do I want to be one. I am a normal person from a normal family. It is you who have not understood anything."

From that moment their attitude changed. I had gained their respect. They began to greet me and smile at me. The photographs had been sufficient. Not that all this had pleased me, but *pazienza!* one must learn to adapt to situations and know how to take advantage of the right moment.

Moreover, their distorted ideas of Arabs may have been the result of the Zionist propaganda found in so many American films: films about the desert, and Egypt, and other places in the Middle East. Films about Israel always told the same story: The Jews went into the desert and made it into a paradise; they brought European civilization—the civilization of the modern world—to the primitive Arabs. And the Arab has always been represented as someone of sinister aspect who kills and steals children. It is simple, elementary propaganda that goes straight to the heart.

I finished the course with high marks and went back to my old passion of reading mystery and adventure stories to improve my German.

Life in Exile

I got to know the life of the foreign students in Vienna, a strange existence that I had never experienced before.

They spent a huge amount of time with their friends. This excited me: to be among so many young men and with Muhammad. Except for the occasional Austrian fiancée, I was always the only woman, so I was fussed over and respected by everyone.

In the afternoons I would usually go to Aida, the meeting place for students from all over the Middle East, or else we would go to one of the numerous Viennese cafés.

The old Viennese cafés were quiet, relaxing places, more suitable for studying than chatting. There were photos on the walls of writers, musicians, actors, and artists who had gone there in search of a calm, secluded spot. If you raised your voice, old ladies would stare at you angrily. The Viennese were very fond of their cafés, maybe because spending a lot of time in their favorite café saved them from turning on the heat at home.

When evening came we would often leave the bars and go to the cinema. After the movies we would eat at one of the all-night restaurants, usually at the Bazaar Grill. I grew to love the place: I liked the checked lace curtains and the kindly waiters. German is often considered a harsh language, but I found it gentle, with delicate, courteous, almost simpering expressions. For example, instead of "Madam" they would say "My dear Madam." There was always a newspaper in the restaurants for anyone to read, something I liked very much.

We used to spend the afternoons discussing politics. Political discussions were our daily bread. We talked about Palestine, the Arab world, the international situation. But the discussions were often dry, or polemical, and did not lead to any real political action. The situation among the Arab students was not simple. Egyptians, Syrians, Iraqis, or Palestinians brought with them their own conflicts, and were not prepared to seek strength in unity. In the end the small amount of political struggle possible in Austria in those years resulted in arid divisions among small groups of students, in which the various embassies intervened. The Palestinians were the most aggressive, as well as the most controlled by their embassy.

People in Vienna at the time were not used to political discussions and protests; the government was very conservative and did not approve of this sort of activity. Everything proceeded calmly and no one protested—as if there were no problems.

The impossibility of having any real influence roused our anguish and frustration, and that was how our evenings often ended. After the political diatribes, my companions would begin to play cards, isolating themselves from me and from the rest of the world. It was deadly boring to spend the evening watching others play cards. In my opinion, playing cards transformed people, revealing them, and stripping them bare. The challenge would reveal their characters and tensions and often lead to quarrels. They would continue until six or even eight o'clock in the morning.

For the most part our life was spent among other foreigners. It was very difficult to get to know well-educated, intellectual people, or even Viennese students. Foreigners were seen as truly bad. We were not allowed to become part of society, but remained marginalized. The most that Arab students could do was make friends with some drunk Austrian in a bar and win some money off him playing cards.

Austrian female students would not think of going out with a foreigner, especially if he were Arab, because they felt superior. So young Arabs could only get to know waitresses, and young women in bars and discotheques. It was not a very interesting world.

My own relationships with young Viennese women were always painful; I was never able to find the deep friendships I had been used to. I found them cold and distant: friendship for them merely consisted of passing the time among groups of young men. Moreover they were somewhat empty-headed—none had the cultural interests that were so basic for me. And they were jealous, because my friends paid more attention to me than to them, especially as we would be speaking in Arabic.

After my initial enthusiasm, I realized how monotonous the days were. We did not talk much about our studies and the university. I felt an emptiness in the lives of my companions in exile and in my own life. The days spent in bars and at home in useless discussions were a waste of time and of our youth—it was a lazy way of life.

I shared my concerns with Muhammad and began refusing to go out. I no longer enjoyed seeing the same faces, talking about the same things, and watching the usual Westerns. I hate Westerns to this day, because they remind me of that period in Vienna when, day after day, life was the same.

I spent a lot of time alone in our horrible apartment or taking long walks in the parks under a perpetually gray sky with an umbrella in my hand. I was studying for the last examination I had to take in Damascus, the history of philosophy. I became familiar with solitude. I was disappointed, betrayed by a reality that I had imagined otherwise.

A Pause for Reflection

Toward the end of 1966 I went to Damascus to finish the course for my degree. My departure resolved for a while the problem of my boredom, which was beginning to get to me. It felt like a vacation to return to the university without the exhaustion of the years when I was working in Kuwait and was only able to take the exams.

I had a great longing to see my parents and my sisters, so I made a quick trip to Palestine. It was my first time back in Nablus in winter after so many years. I had been used to living in Kuwait for so long, where it was always summer and where you could not enjoy the marvelous change of seasons. I had almost forgotten what a Palestinian winter was like, with its tepid sun and pouring rain and everything dry again within half an hour. We spent the time in the house, sitting around the wood-burning stove, our heat source, chatting and roasting chestnuts, eating cheese and bread dipped in our own olive oil and drinking the juice of oranges and grapefruits from our land. My school friends came to visit and I was enthusiastic about everything around me. I made the others laugh at my pleasure over every little thing, at my attention to details they no longer noticed.

My mother treated me as an equal for the first time. I was married, I was a woman, I was no longer a young girl and she took me much more seriously. It was so great to have this new relationship with her. She spoiled me, paid me a lot of attention, and kept giving me things to eat because I had lost weight. She was worried that we students did not have enough money to spend on food. I thoroughly enjoyed the atmosphere at home, in my town, and in Palestine.

Unfortunately I could not enjoy this pleasure for long. The political situation was explosive—relations between Jordan and Syria were very tense, and there were constant strikes and demonstrations. The schools had been closed and the streets were full of soldiers. The Syrian and Jordanian armies were massed at their respective borders and the frontiers were said to be closed from one moment to the next. I had to catch my plane to Vienna from Damascus, so in order not to risk getting delayed in Nablus for who knows how long, I had to cut short my wonderful stay.

The journey and my distance from Vienna were a test of my feelings for Muhammad. I felt enormous nostalgia and longing to return and see him again. This time, however, the flight to Vienna was different. My expectations, my dreams, my thoughts were no longer the same: I had grown up and no longer deluded myself. I knew the hard reality awaiting me.

My meeting with Muhammad was emotional and wonderful. Life in Vienna resumed the same as before.

My disillusionment and loneliness were even greater. I felt a failure, betrayed, marginalized.

My sister sent me a telegram to say I had passed the last exam and now had my degree. I had handed in my thesis prior to taking the final exams, as was the custom at the university in Damascus, so I thought I had all the necessary papers to enroll in my specialty in Vienna. Then I discovered that I would need to pass an exam in Latin to validate my degree. This rule had been abolished some years before I had enrolled at the university in Damascus. I was disappointed but decided to make the effort.

The Second Disaster

The war of 1967, the so-called Six-Day War, struck like a bolt of lightning. My private anguish disappeared in the face of this great tragedy. It was a fatal blow and we were paralyzed.

The news united all the Arabs. We were shut up in our squalid little rooms, in silence, day and night, 24 hours after 24 hours, glued to the radio. We tried to get Radio London or the Egyptian radio. We sought news any way we could, because Austrian newspapers did not pay much attention to politics. They praised the miraculous success of the Israeli army and despised the "worms" who had been dispatched in six days. An armed Israel, supported by America, had occupied part of Syria, Egypt, Jordan and all of Gaza, while Europe—this civilized Europe—remained silent.

Our eyes were red with crying and exhaustion. We could not get news of our loved ones; all contact had been broken. We were destroyed. No one spoke, no one ate. We were turned to stone, desperate, impotent.

Those of us who were abroad lost the right to return. We were cut off, foreigners, nobodies. Once again we had lost everything. We were without land, home or support. It was unbearable to feel oneself an orphan for the second time. Jaffa and Nablus were blurred in my mind; I felt the grief of being separated from them both. I don't know which separation was the worst, that of Jaffa, because I never understood it, or that of Nablus, which I understood too well.

Of my family, only my two youngest sisters, my brother Ihsan, and my parents were in Palestine when the war broke out. Adnan was in Libya, Issam in Spain, and my other three sisters were at the universities of Jordan and Syria. They too were cut off and lost the right to return.

Muhammad's family was also away from Palestine, in Saudi Arabia, in 1967, so they lost everything yet again. They were never able to return to their home in Nablus and for them it was a great tragedy. Over the years and at great sacrifice they have succeeded in building a beautiful residence in Jordan—not in Saudi Arabia, because they were not allowed to stay there permanently. But no one feels at home, even now. When they talk of "our home" they mean the house in Nablus. The elderly father's greatest dream is to die in his own home and be buried in Nablus.

This tragedy affected many Palestinian families. There were huge acts of rebellion. When the Israelis took the census to establish who was "absent," some women managed to take children from other families and pass them off as their own in place of those who were abroad. Because they mistrusted the soldiers, they wanted to ensure that their children could return home.

When we finally reestablished contact with our families and were able to exchange letters and telephone calls, the news we heard was tragic. They told us of the humiliation of having soldiers in the streets making all the decisions, destroying houses, imprisoning people or deporting them and seizing their property.

We felt not only grief for our enormous loss, but anger and disappointment. The war had been lost without ever being fought, not only because of America's unlimited economic and military support for Israel, but also because of the lack of commitment and the political inadequacy of all the Arab countries. Syria was more concerned with protecting its own border with Jordan than with confronting the Israeli armies in the Golan. The Jordanian army had been given orders to retreat. We Palestinians did not have the strength to defend ourselves and we were abandoned by the Jordanian government. Still, there were also many stories of heroism among the Palestinian officials in the Jordanian army who refused to obey orders to retreat and went on fighting to the end, giving their lives in a desperate effort to defend every single centimeter of our land.

The behavior of the Arab countries was further proof that they were only puppet regimes, defending their own interests and not those of the people. The biggest disappointment was over Nasser's Egypt. The Israelis had destroyed all the Egyptian military planes on the ground at the airports, before they could even take off. The planes had not been concealed or protected, and the soldiers had been abandoned to their fate without ever knowing what they should do. This military failure showed that Nasser had not been capable of choosing his ministers: he had been tricked and betrayed by his own collaborators. It was proof of political inadequacy. When he closed the Suez Canal to Israeli ships he should have anticipated a war and been prepared to face up to it. Instead, even though he was primarily a military rather than a political leader, he had not risen to the challenge.

He was, after all, the only Arab leader who enjoyed some of our respect—the only one who had shown any real support for our cause. He was obliged to step down, but there was no one in line to replace him. It was the collapse of a myth. Shortly afterward, the Ba'ath party collapsed for us as well.

The dream of Arab unity was over. Egypt was defeated. The Ba'ath party in Syria and Iraq had been compromised like all those that had preceded it. The Six-Day War changed everything.

This is why the generation after ours, those born around 1967, is so different. Israel, for them, is a reality with which they have lived since they were born; they are extremely aware of the situation and have no illusions about the Arab countries. They know that they are alone and that is why they gather in the squares and fight the occupation themselves, with whatever means they have. As for us, we had so many dreams, so many words and ideologies. We believed in socialism and in pan-Arabism. Today everything is different.

The war had turned our lives upside down, and our grief dragged on for many months.

As we began to wake up from the nightmare, the worst happened: Nasser died. And our lives had to go on. Some said he was assassinated, others that he had had a heart attack. I remember crying a great deal. I wept for the man and I wept for the end of my hopes, for my youth spent believing in an ideal. The death of Nasser was the end of a dream; it was a political and a human loss, the onset of desperation. The epoch of myths had come to an end, and something in me began to die, something young, fresh, and intense. It became entangled with my personal desperation and dissatisfaction with my life. I cried day and night.

Children and Disaster

Some time later I discovered that I was pregnant. It was a very emotional moment. My first child. He had not been planned; we had never discussed it. I had conceived in the excitement of being together again after my brief stay in Palestine. I had been so happy to see my husband that I relaxed and never gave it a thought.

I wanted this child; I had always wanted to have a son. I thought I would be able to send him to a nursery in Vienna and continue with my studies. He would already be big by the time we went home.

But a child is a big responsibility. We even talked about a possible abortion. It was against the law in Vienna, but one could go to Czechoslovakia. We decided immediately that it was out of the question. I, in particular, was determined to keep the child. Despite the uncertainty of the future, the journey ahead of us, and the tragedy that had befallen us, I was not afraid.

Sultan was born that October. He was a wonderful child who filled me with joy. He made me feel so proud to have created—not just accommodated, as some would say—a new life. It was a profound experience that men cannot understand. It is a purely feminine experience that makes one stronger, more responsible, brighter, more able to bear pain, and to give even more.

But my life had changed. The tragedy of the war had marked us. We continued to live among all these friends who were sad and anguished. We smoked and slept and ate little. Vienna was cold and our room was always closed and smoky.

My baby Sultan had to put up with the smoky, anguished atmosphere in which we were immersed every day. When he was little more than three months, he fell ill. He refused to eat and vomited everything. I told myself it was an illness caused by irritability. His stomach contracted and he needed an operation. Scarcely born and he was already a victim of an unjust world.

After the war, life in Vienna had become hell for us Palestinians and for all Middle Easterners. The racism was so aggressive that we were afraid to go out in the streets. Just to have slightly dark skin and black hair was reason enough to be threatened and attacked. Sometimes Middle Easterners were beaten. Why? Because we had lost the war? Because we were weak? We had shown that we did not deserve respect. In the cafés, on the street, in restaurants, everywhere, were provocative laughs. The victors were greatly admired and their strength and military success extolled.

I experienced racism even in little things. Sultan was growing, so I would take him to the park. He was a lively child who ran and jumped and played. The Austrians would get annoyed and say he should be controlled. "These people from the Third World don't know how to raise their children!" If his ball landed on the lawn it was a tragedy; stepping on the grass to retrieve it, a sacrilege. The old people, who considered themselves the guardians of the country, would interfere and retrieve the ball with long iron poles.

Even the shopkeepers were cold toward us. You could go to the same store every day for a year, and yet, if you were short five pennies they would not give you what you needed, even though they knew perfectly well that they would see you again the next day.

My own landlord only saw his children about once a year, even though they actually lived in Vienna. I felt sorry for him when his wife died and he was left alone. His children did not invite him for Christmas, so I called him and prepared a big feast. He arrived with a piece of candy for the baby—one piece, rather than a box of candies, even though he was a very rich man. And he was not in the least embarrassed. I refused to be like that.

I remember, too, the fiancée of a friend who often came to see me because she worked in an office near my house. I would offer her a tart or a dessert, and she would be amazed and want to pay me! Despite being the only daughter of a fairly well-off mother, she was used to bringing her own food when she visited her people. They would sit down at the table and each one would have his own food in front of him. I was dumbfounded by such arid relationships, which they found perfectly natural. She was struck by my generosity. Can you imagine? Every day I would give her something, and she was never able to understand why.

It was hard enough before the war to live in such a hostile country—imagine what it was like when we had lost everything. In time, life became even more difficult. Just surviving was an enormous problem—we no longer received money from home and had to manage without it.

Muhammad tried to find some work, and in the summer he went to work in Germany while I stayed alone with the baby. Those were sad, grievous times.

Muhammad's work did not always provide enough to support our family. We had a Persian rug that someone had given us and a tape recorder. Every month we would take them to the pawnshop—this was the custom in Vienna—they would give us money for them and then when we had money again, we would retrieve our possessions. This happened almost every month, just like a job.

The months in Vienna went by in the same sad way. We Palestinians could not manage to be happy. I remember once deciding to celebrate New Year's and be carefree, just for once. We went to the Wiener Wald in Grinzing. Over time I had learned to enjoy those places, to appreciate the warmth of all that wood and sense the joy and liveliness. I left the baby at home alone, asking a neighbor to keep an eye on him. I wanted to spend an evening without cares. We went out in a crowd with the intention of enjoying ourselves. We swore not to talk politics or about our country, but only of happy, carefree things. We ate, and played at being happy. But in the end, almost everyone got drunk, and we began to talk politics, to argue and raise our voices. When it was time to go home, we were almost in tears.

So I understood that we were a people condemned to be without joy. We did not have time for pleasure. We had experienced one tragedy after another, with families split up, and we lived far from home. We always had to endure both psychological and physical oppression that has prevented us from learning how to be happy, from learning how to spend a simple, carefree evening. The entire Palestinian population in exile seemed to me then to have this one thing in common: we did not know how to enjoy ourselves.

The only light in the dark for me was the opera. Fortunately the theater was close to our apartment and I could go there on foot, alone, even at night. Muhammad would stay home with the baby. None of our friends wanted to go; even if one of them liked music he would not admit to it. That meant being westernized, losing one's identity, forgetting one's origin. In fact they all made fun of me, calling me "the Philosopher." I hated this attitude of theirs, this fear of change that seemed typical of the Arab students.

I spent hours of pure joy there. I was in paradise, and during those moments Vienna and the whole world became splendid. I saw *Aida, Carmen, Tosca, La Traviata,* and I saw the *Swan Lake* ballet. I went to hear the Vienna Philharmonic directed by Herbert von Karajan: Beethoven symphonies, Tchaikovsky, Wagner, Mozart, and Vivaldi concertos. I floated on air. It was a divine feeling; I was entering a world of magic. I would return home with my hands red from clapping. I held that warmth, that magical atmosphere, inside me for a whole week. Outside, unfortunately, there was still the cold world filled with loneliness, disappointment, bitterness, and uncertainty about the future.

I had always imagined a different life, desired it almost scientifically, constructed it moment by moment. I would have reached up and touched the sky, had I the chance of achieving what I had always dreamed. All this was crushed.

I spent endless hours alone with Sultan in our miserable apartment. Muhammad was always away at work and the months he was in Germany were terrible. It was humiliating to think that the economic situation would be resolved only when money started to arrive again from home. I had to stay with our child, so I could not work and had to abandon my field of specialization. My dreams were disappearing, and even the economic independence that I had won for myself in Kuwait no longer existed.

My life was suspended between my husband and my son; I felt the huge weight of responsibility with no room left for myself. I had absolutely lost my independence. I understood for the first time that when a woman marries she loses the right to create her own life, her destiny, to make decisions about the present and the future. I felt that marriage tied women down, imprisoned them, left them powerless, and erased their needs.

In the silence of my days I thought and thought about a solution. I was convinced that doing everything possible to continue to study was our little piece of land. But after the war and the birth of our baby and the necessity of working, the situation was so complicated that such a solution became improbable.

Everyone's existence was gloomy. I was surrounded by darkness and distrust. Life seemed to have no more meaning. The days were all the same without the slightest change, always the same rhythm. Vienna was like a witch who drugged her inhabitants, slowly, with an elixir that prevented them from thinking and reacting, that paralyzed them and even pleased them with the monotony of the days. I could see no solution; it was a tunnel with no end.

I vegetated, I was passive, lifeless, fading away. Alone in a world of crushed dreams I felt powerless, defeated, a prisoner. I could not move mountains as I had thought; I could change nothing and no one. Everything I had ever believed in came under question.

I wanted to shut myself away and hide. I broke off all contact with my friends in Kuwait, Syria, the United States, and the Occupied Territories. I was too sad and did not want them to see my weakness. I told my family that I was fine, that everything was going well, and that I was happy. I could not add my pain to theirs; besides, I thought I ought to be able to solve my own problems.

The only person that I wrote to and asked advice of was my brother Issam. He was, at that time, my best friend and I opened up to him without embarrassment. Ever since our life together in Nablus, our relationship had been one of complicity. Adnan was like a boss, and Issam like a co-worker—approachable, easy to talk to. He was living in Madrid. After saving some money, he had had the courage to leave Kuwait and go to Spain to get a degree in political science.

Something wonderful happened: he came to see me in Vienna. Those were delightful days. He calmed me, telling me that my problems were shared by all the students and that I should be thinking first and foremost of my family. His presence, his affection, his friendship, and his advice warmed my heart amid the cold of Vienna.

Adnan also came to see me from Lebanon. Our reconciliation after so many years was beautiful. The political power of the Ba'ath party had begun to annoy the Emir of Kuwait, so Adnan's paper had been closed down and he was asked to leave the country. He wanted to get to know my husband whom he had never met, and see my son and, of course, to be with me. Those were wonderful days, full of emotional conversations and a great peace. My husband had heard about Adnan from me and from others, and he was impressed with his tremendous culture, gentleness, and depth.

After my brothers left, I was once again surrounded by silence and emptiness. But after this precious time with them I began to understand my problem. During the months I had spent in Vienna I had gone on comparing my husband, my friends, and the life of exile with the myth that I had created and fixed in my mind. During the two years of my engagement, I had idealized matrimony and the image of Vienna. I had put too much confidence in myself and my strength and ability to understand and change the world. I had thought that an individual could create his or her own destiny. This is not always true.

Early in 1969 I discovered that I was pregnant for a second time. It was something we really did not want—yet another difficulty to add to the thousands of others. The pregnancy seemed illogical, absurd, and very serious. It was the result of a lack of sexual understanding. There were arguments that we were afraid to confront. But within me, I wanted to have another child and dreamed possibly of a girl. I had always wished for a large family, so these mistakes also made me happy and grateful. We had many misgivings but in the end we decided to keep the baby.

My daughter was born in October of 1969. I called her Ruba which means "a hill in flower." She was a splendid little bundle, so beautiful she made me cry. I could not believe that I had a daughter; it was a tremendous feeling. I hugged her and said: "This is my daughter, this is my friend, this is my treasure, this is me." I had always wanted a daughter and had tried to imagine what life with a little girl would be like—a different experience from having a boy. My husband, too, was happy. I thanked my inexperience for allowing me to have this gift.

Decisions

Ruba's birth brought me new worries, but also fresh energy. Now more than ever I could not tolerate the death of my present and my future. I had to react. I refused to remain suffocated and immersed in the slow drug that was Vienna, in that vicious cycle of powerlessness and loneliness. I searched for a solution. We needed a total change, a new demanding and constructive beginning. Perhaps we needed to leave Vienna.

I hated this city where nothing ever happened, no one protested, no one went on strike, no one took action, where everything was apparently perfect, but where people were colder than snow. I hated Vienna where the sun never shone, gray Vienna, Vienna where no faces were familiar and no one ever smiled. I hated Vienna as the symbol of my failure. I could not even see its beauty. I would often go for walks in the gardens with my children or visit buildings and monuments, but they no longer interested me.

I thought it would be good to go somewhere new and put the past behind me. I did not want to spend any more time in waiting, I wanted to act and not leave my life up to fate. I no longer listened when people told me to wait, have patience, that with time everything would be better. I kept insisting to Muhammad and finally managed to convince him. Away from Vienna, I too would be able to study my specialty. We began to write to universities in Holland, the United States, and Canada. We did not consider the Arab countries because we could only return to them when we had succeeded and achieved something. No one can return home in defeat, crushed with the weight of failure.

At that time we had a visit from Muhammad's brother, who was studying medicine in Italy and had married an Italian. He told us about Italy and the simple, happy people there. He spoke about Parma, a small, gentle city, green, with a mild climate. He told us that it was easy to live there and that the people could be trusted. Italy seemed to me like paradise, just what we needed.

We began to think about moving there. Why not? Admittedly, there was the problem of language, but we were encouraged by the presence of a family member. After the war, it was particularly important to be near someone in our family—we needed that warmth, affection, and security.

It was best for one of us to go take a look at the country and the city in order to have a better idea what awaited us and whether we could transfer to the university. Muhammad went and returned enthusiastic. He said the language was easy and that the prospects of living were acceptable. He also reported that it was very different from Vienna and he laughed and was happy as he said it.

It was no longer possible for me to be as enthusiastic as

I had once been about a new life, but I certainly could not live any longer in Vienna. I knew that it would help us to change location, but I was also aware that true change had to come from within. We made our decision. We would move to Italy.

It was a shock for our friends—a revolution, an explosion in the sick atmosphere of Vienna. It was something that rarely happened. Some students, of course, graduated and succeeded, but for the most part they were paralyzed and trapped in a kind of spell. They greatly admired and envied our courage. They told us that it was great what we were doing, the best thing possible... but they remained stuck, closed in, incapable of escaping themselves.

One evening in March 1970, after parties and celebrations, our friends accompanied us to the train. Muhammad, Sultan, Ruba, and I left for Italy.

FIVE

Italy
1970–1992

A New Life

It was the first time I had traveled by train. I liked it very
much—it was comfortable and spacious. It was possible to
get up, walk around, and communicate. There were both
young and old on the train; so many new faces and different
types fascinated me. Some Italians turned to us and began
speaking. I looked at them happily but could not understand
what they were saying. Muhammad kept telling me to look at
the countryside out the window. The woods and fields
between Austria and Italy are very beautiful. There were so
many new stations and cities whose names I had never heard.
My head was spinning, and the train made me feel a little
sick; when I looked out of the window it felt as if the trees
were moving. Muhammad teased me and was very amused. I
found the situation funny, and tried not to look out.

We had left our ugly, miserable, cold apartment in
Vienna. We brought with us only a few things and the

television that we had purchased. That was an important object and we did not want to leave it behind.

My mind was full of a thousand thoughts. I had gone to Vienna filled with dreams and expectations of happiness; I had thought I had the world in the palm of my hand. I left there, discouraged and embittered, but also ready for a new undertaking, a new country, a new language, without any great dreams or plans, except to change and go forward.

I was leaving Vienna with a boy of almost two and a half and a little bundle that was my daughter. I held her tight, cuddled her in my arms. I was truly happy, though I don't know why; it seemed such a wonderful thing to have a baby. I imagined her growing up, thought about her education and my relationship with her. At the same time I was assailed by the fear of not being up to it, of not being able to help her avoid life's difficulties. On the other hand, I was convinced that difficulties helped build personality, and that it would not be right for a child to arrive in the world and find everything in its place, and nothing left to manage. That would not allow for growth. So I told myself: Everyone must take up his cross and go on; I will do my part and see what happens.

I was leaving Vienna with a man who loved me a great deal. Even though he and I were very different, it was very important to me to be with him. His presence made me happy.

I thought about Italy and what was ahead of me, but at the same time I tried not to think too much. I had already been disappointed once and did not want to give way to dreams. I had never been to Italy, so I had no idea what to expect. For me Italy was macaroni. I had read Alberto Moravia's *The Woman of Rome* and *Time of Indifference*. I had read Leopardi and Pirandello, whom I liked very much.

I had also read a few things about Venice and knew that it was a fascinating city, full of mysteries. But I had also learned that what you gather from books is different from what you learn through experience.

When we arrived in Parma, my brother-in-law was there to meet us and take us to a hotel in the city center. At last I found again the warm sun of spring. There were so many people on the go: young men joking around and calling out to each other, a lively market that reminded me of the center of Nablus. Everything was different from somber, silent, rainy Vienna.

We sat down at a café in the Piazza Garibaldi, and then we went along some little streets with shops, buildings, and gardens. The lump in my throat dissolved rapidly. I lost the sensation of being small, a zero: I felt like a person again, and not in the least like a foreigner. I continued to look around, and everything pleased me.

The elegance of the people and the suits worn by the young men impressed me. In Vienna we saw everything but elegance. People were white, fair, soap and water, and the young women never wore make-up. I put kohl on my eyes because it is an Arab tradition used by all our women. It is done to protect the eyes, but also to make us beautiful and emphasize our dark eyes. To wear make-up and dress elegantly is a sign that you care about yourself, that you feel a desire to improve. These little details all contributed to putting me at ease.

We spent our first few days in the hotel. We often ate in restaurants full of noisy people who reminded me of our guests at home. We had come far from silent Vienna, where you were not supposed to leave the table or look at the people around you. I felt the cold melt, and the fog that had encircled me for so long, vanish. I began to come alive again. I was enthusiastic about everything. I remember

I kept repeating, "I like it, I really like it, I think I can live in this country."

We could not continue to live in the hotel with a little baby. Also, it was rather expensive and our means were limited. Our brother-in-law had rented a house for us but it was not yet available. So a friend decided to let us use his apartment temporarily, a very generous gesture. We moved to that little house, into a kind of attic, pretty, clean, very old but pleasant. I felt really good there— everything seemed full of life.

My husband immediately began to attend the university. I stayed home alone and so had to get along and make contact with people. Our house was situated in an old, old street in the heart of Parma, near Via Garibaldi, an area of little streets full of stores and activity.

Every day I went to the vegetable store where there was a very kind lady. I did not know how to speak Italian, so I expressed myself with signs. That lady's smile when she saw me for the first time and understood my difficulties moved me so much. I did not know how to add up the money and she helped. During the entire five years I had spent in Vienna I had not once seen such a smile or encountered such helpfulness.

The shop still exists and I saw the lady again a few weeks ago, after a gap of some 21 years. She recognized me, even though I have changed, grown thinner, and cut my hair. And she asked about my children. She told me that her sons were married and were working with her. She said, "It is so nice that you are an Italian now." A meeting of old friends. I adore these relationships, this spontaneous, sincere communication. Many Italians tell me that I describe an Italy that they don't know; that all things are not so wonderful in Italy. But this is what my life has been.

I learned to like coffee in Italy. I like the idea that you could be nearly anywhere and decide to enter a café for a short rest, sit down at a table, or stay just a few minutes. I have always enjoyed reading a newspaper while I drink a cup of coffee, in my kitchen or in my bedroom, but also outdoors, among people, chatting with a friend. I liked this custom and so I often went to a bar. It was so easy to say "Coffee!" and to buy an ice cream for my son—I just had to point to a picture.

Ever since I was a young girl I had been fascinated by such places. I had read a book by a Lebanese writer, Suheil Idriss, called *The Latin Quarter*, about the area in Paris where students and intellectuals live. I spent hours dreaming about such a life of freedom, with its encounters in cafés and streets. The bar provided me an opportunity to leave the house; it gave me a sense of freedom. I used to pass in front of those cafés for men only in Nablus and sometimes felt the urge to sit down myself and watch the passersby.

I like to sit in Italian cafés, where everyone speaks loudly, and listen to people's stories. My husband thinks this is a weakness of mine. He had lived in Austria since he was a little boy and was used to being very discreet, speaking in a low voice, lowering the volume of the television. It is a constant battle between us. In Vienna it was not possible to increase the volume of the television, whereas in Italy there was no need even to turn it on, since we could hear the one next door so clearly. For years in Parma I woke to the sound of the radio next door.

A Real Home

Several months later, our apartment became available. Once again we gathered our belongings and moved. The house was on Via Solferino, a tree-lined street with elegant two- and three-story apartment buildings surrounded by gardens. It was very different from the apartment in which I had begun my married life. It was a real home, roomy with lots of windows. Everywhere I turned I could see the green foliage. The rooms were empty, but that did not bother me.

We only had the television set that we had brought with us from Vienna. We put it on a chair in our large living room. That important television set, sitting in the middle of the room, made it look like a film director's house. We began to buy the furniture we needed, a little at a time.

Luckily I had saved my severance pay from work in Kuwait and this made it possible to have a decent beginning, even though, of course, we were not living in luxury. Muhammad found some work and they were once again sending us money from home.

But it was not easy to receive the money. We got to know the Italian *sciopero*: train strikes, public transportation strikes, postal strikes. The delays provoked by these demonstrations seemed endless. These strikes left a bad impression on me. In our country, strikes were an achievement, something we worked hard and prepared for, an extremely important moment of political and social struggle, during which everything came to a halt and for which we risked a great deal, even arrest or injury. In Italy it seemed too easy, like a game, or a day's vacation; there was none of the atmosphere that I thought should accompany protests.

We were the only foreign family in our neighborhood. Our unusual presence caused a lot of stir, and people were very curious to learn that we were Arabs.

The people I met near my house or on the street or in stores greeted me with smiles. I only needed to nod my head. Relations were nice and easy. Some people would talk to me, even though I did not understand, just like on the train when we were traveling to Italy; evidently it was part of the Italian character.

Because I had to manage on my own, without my husband's help, I got to know people and learned a lot. I always took Sultan with me wherever I went, to the dairy, the tobacconist, or the bakery, but Ruba, who was very small, I left at home. This roused the curiosity of our neighbors, who began to think that something was wrong. I did not take Ruba with me simply because I did not have a stroller and I would not have been able to do the shopping with her in my arms.

One day, a woman who could not resist her curiosity any longer knocked on my door to find out what mystery was hiding behind our walls, whether there were babies or Martians. She came with a gift, something for the house, and told me that, if I needed, I could leave the baby with her whenever I wanted. She was an elderly woman who lived in my apartment building, with her grown-up son. I explained to her about the stroller and why I could not take my baby out with me.

Word spread. Several days later, an American woman, the wife of an Italian cardiologist who lived in our building, came to find me and gave me her daughter's stroller, which she did not need any more. With the problem of the stroller resolved, the mystery of the baby who always stayed at home was cleared up. Everyone would stop to look at her in the streets; she was a chubby little girl with dark hair and dark eyes. She looked like a doll and was liked by everyone, especially because she looked so different.

I would go to the park with the children and slowly I began to learn Italian and make friends with other young women. They called me *la signora gentile* (the nice lady)— they seemed to think me a "normal" foreigner. Who knows why; perhaps they thought foreigners were ignorant, untidy, uncivilized, or backward. And so when they saw a "nice" foreigner—presentable, with two children—they were attracted, fascinated. In any case, I too was charmed by their helpfulness.

The old men we met in the street or in the park made me laugh. As soon as they saw me, they would say, "You know, I've been to the Middle East, too" or "I've been to Libya" or "I was once in Somalia." I would answer: "And what's that to do with me? I am from a different country. Asia, Jerusalem, Christ. I have nothing to do with Libya or Somalia."

They were very confused and perhaps a little ignorant, but they were all affectionate, and kept candies in their pocket for the children. It was great to meet those smiling faces.

I began going to the gardens with Rosalba, a woman who lived in my building. She was married to a surgeon and had a daughter of more or less the same age as my children and was expecting another child. She knew a little English and so we were able to communicate, and she was very generous with me. I learned later that she came from the South and knew what it meant to be alone and far from her land and her own family. She understood and could imagine my feelings, my suffering, and my loneliness and offered me her friendship. She wanted to help soften difficult experiences that she too had had to confront.

I was very moved by Rosalba's generosity and her willingness, at any time, to lend a hand with anything. She is a person who makes herself available unconditionally at a moment's notice. We have remained friends for twenty years. More than a friend, she became a sister, a person with whom I had daily contact and who has always stood by me in the most difficult and grievous times.

This warmth made it easier to tackle the most difficult situations and renewed my hopes.

I had only one problem: I felt too much like a mother, a wife, a housewife, and I had never wanted that. I still dreamed about studying child psychology, it was my *idée fixe*. But there was no course in my specialty at the University of Parma. The place to go was Bologna, which would be very difficult—I would have to leave my two children, and it was so expensive. My husband was continuing his studies. He was always away from home, taking courses at the university. Once again, I was the one to make the sacrifice and give up my plans. I tried to persuade myself that it was only fair, that my husband and children came first; I told myself that I could study my specialization at any time. I was trying to convince myself, but I was not very happy about it.

I would have liked to have studied Italian but unfortunately there wasn't any school for foreigners in Parma. So I learned to speak Italian by going into stores and being with people. Muhammad, on the other hand, studied books written in Italian and attended lessons at the university, which is why his Italian is more correct than mine. Everyone thinks he is Italian when they hear him speak.

During my first months in Parma, something again happened to disturb me. I thought I was pregnant for the third time. I really did not want to be. It was neither the right moment nor the right event. What is more, this time I had taken precautions, having learned from my previous experience, and I thought I was safe.

What to do? Look for a gynecologist? Whom could I talk to about it? A Palestinian or Arab student? It didn't seem the right sort of help. I didn't know what to do and I was very worried by the possibility of pregnancy. I talked with Rosalba about it.

She wrote down the address of her doctor for me. Fortunately he understood German, even though he could not speak it; the most important thing for me was to be understood. What he had to tell me was easy to understand: yes or no. And it was yes. I was three months pregnant. I was stunned.

At first it was hard to accept. I foresaw so many difficulties. Logically it was crazy, but my feelings kept telling me that three children were a great gift and that actually I had always wanted a large family.

A wonderful son was born in October 1970. He was splendid, with blue eyes, and he made me so happy. I called him Ra'ed. He was healthy and beautiful as an angel. I thanked God a hundred times for that precious gift. And so out of ignorance, lack of sexual knowledge, and naivete, I had made a family. It would have been more sensible to have planned it, but then I might never have had children—the right moment might never have occurred. My neighbors from then on called me "the lady with all those children."

Journey to Palestine

After 1967, the only contact I had had with my family were letters and telephone conversations. I kept dreaming about going home so that my children would get to know my parents and the grandparents would meet their grandchildren. My children were the first grandchildren in the family and everyone would be excited to see them. I began to think about it seriously. I knew that I would only be granted a month's pass to go home and that I would have to apply as if I were a foreigner.

In 1972, I made up my mind and left with my three children. Sultan was five, Ruba three, and Ra'ed two.

We arrived in Amman and stayed there a few days, just long enough to get the required documents for entering the Occupied Territories. My sister put us up and she and a friend showed us around the city. But with three children it was very tiring and I could not relax. My attention was entirely focused on that day when I would cross the border. It would be the first time that I had to cross the Allenby Bridge in order to go home. I knew that it was an extremely difficult experience for all of us Palestinians. First you have to go through Jordanian customs and then the nearby Israeli checkpoint. It was difficult to say which was worse, they were both so horrible. But our humiliation at the hands of the Israelis was overwhelming.

Our day of departure arrived. My sister came with us to the border. It was very hot and there was a huge crowd. We managed to get through the Jordanian checkpoint. Then followed a long wait under the fierce sun. The children were tired and thirsty but the water we had brought was boiling.

Our turn finally came. The Israeli soldiers took away all my possessions: my handbag, my suitcases, my clothes and shoes. They strip-searched me. Ruba was hugging her doll, her treasure; she was very proud of it because it could sing and speak. Suddenly one of the soldiers jerked it out of her arms. Ruba tried to hold on to it, and began to cry.

The policeman began ripping up the doll, searching to see if there were something hidden in it. I was furious. I asked the soldier whether he didn't have children himself, whether he had no pity, whether he thought it was acceptable to treat children like this. He answered that we were not people, not human beings, that he could do whatever he liked and certainly did not intend to listen to any criticism from me.

I wanted to file an official complaint, but the way people stared at me convinced me that it would be useless and that this sort of violence and harshness was the rule.

I felt wounded, humiliated. They wanted to deny us our basic rights. But no force on earth, no politics could convince me that this was not my home, the land where I had grown up, where my parents and sisters lived. For many years after that Ruba thought of the Israelis as the bad people who had destroyed her doll. She was in shock for a long time as a result of what happened that day.

The searches over, we were allowed to enter Palestine. We took one of the few buses going to Nablus. It was full, with no room to rest one's feet or breathe. It was almost tragic for such little children.

Finally we arrived home and all the humiliations and exhaustion were forgotten. So many years had gone by. We were so happy. We were overjoyed, and we celebrated and had unforgettable moments. It was so moving to watch the grandparents meet their grandchildren; the children for the first time were surrounded by people who fussed over them, took them for walks, loved them, and talked with them. They had been without grandparents, uncles, and aunts all their lives. This meeting was an extraordinary occasion for them.

Except for the joy of being home again, of being in the arms of my family, the situation in Palestine felt truly tragic. Whenever I met relatives, friends, or neighbors, I heard nothing but talk of people who had been imprisoned or killed, whose homes had been destroyed or land seized.

People's stories, and what I saw for myself, pained me and made me not want to listen or look. I felt helpless, unable to react. What hurt the Palestinians most were the enormous taxes that we had to pay to Israel, the land seizure, and the destruction of houses; many people ended up living in tents and barracks.

The Palestinians resisted and rebelled in whatever way they could: leaflets, strikes, and even occasional attacks. Theirs was a secret, organized struggle. They no longer believed in the promises made by the Arab countries, they were no longer taken in, but continued to struggle on their own. Resistance to the Israeli occupation had begun immediately, especially in the cities. Nothing was known about this struggle abroad, especially in Europe, where Israel was considered a heroic, ideal country, and no one really knew anything about Palestine and the Palestinians.

We heard about many arrests. The stories were all the same: A house suddenly surrounded by dozens of soldiers, armed to the teeth, who broke down the doors and entered, turning everything upside down, striking out, searching for people to arrest. Then they would take someone at random who happened be in the house, leaving the old people, the parents, behind, terrorized and in despair over such violence.

I went to the trial of a 14-year-old boy. The trial was ridiculous: everything was carried out as if the defendant were not there. They decided everything—accusation and condemnation. The spectators were disoriented by such a farce. I came away totally stunned. Of course the boy was found guilty; they sentenced him to eight years in prison. By chance I learned that he is still alive and continuing his fight.

There was a lot of talk about the prisons, some of it terrifying and some fascinating. They said that the walls were full of writings praising Palestine, messages written by the prisoners with the only thing they had—their blood. The walls of the prisons were whitewashed nearly every day to cover up the writing. But of course they could not take blood away from people and so the Israeli soldiers kept on erasing and the prisoners kept on writing.

We, too, were affected by the arrogance of the Israelis. Only Mama, Papa, Nadia, and Badia were at home. Ihsan was in prison, accused of protesting against the occupation and the taxes. He had married recently, and his wife, a charming young teacher with blond hair and green eyes, was pregnant. He had been sent to one of the farthest prisons, in the Negev desert.

My father was shattered by grief. He was allowed to visit him once a month and lived for that day. By now my father was a tired, old man with a heart condition; he was very dear to me with his delicate face, splendid eyes, white hair, and bushy beard.

He went for one of his visits, while I was at home. I remember him getting up at three in the morning, taking pastries, clothes, and mail and leaving the house. The bus ride to the prison took almost twelve hours, and there was no guarantee that he would see Ihsan. If my brother had been put in isolation or there were some other reason, rational or irrational, my father might arrive and not be allowed to see him.

In fact, on that particular occasion he was not. I remember the disappointment and anger of that elderly man, returning home without being able to speak to his son. I felt my heart breaking and I cried silently. My mother would also weep to see him so distraught. But he did not weep—he embodied a father's grief and a man's impotence in the face of an unjust military power. In him could be seen the entire family story, the marks of all our sufferings and struggles. He was a tired father who deserved a monument to his courage, to his patience, and to his resistance, for all that had taken place.

When we were sitting on the veranda one afternoon he told me about the journey he had made to Jaffa in 1967, when, after nineteen years, the frontier between the 1948 Palestine and the West Bank was open for the first time. Like so many Palestinians, my father's first thought was to go see his house, his office, and his property. There were so many families trying to reunite, searching for relatives that they had left behind. For the most part it was a distressing experience.

With great ingenuity, my father took the key he had always kept hanging on a wall in our house, and left for Jaffa. Evidently our neighborhood had not changed. Heart in mouth, he found our house. He gazed at the garden, the wall, the window. He stood there, turned to stone, not knowing whether to go forward or turn back, until someone approached him. At that moment my father understood it was no longer his house. The new tenants were suspicious when they saw this man standing in front of their house. During those months, many other unknown people stood gazing similarly in front of houses in Jaffa. They said: "Excuse me, what do you want? Why are you staring like that?" He answered: "This used to be my house." And they: "It is no longer yours—go away." Sadly my father left.

He went in search of his office, the street where he used to work. Everything there had changed. Lots of new houses had been built. He left and turned toward the sea to feel again what he used to feel long ago. But even the sea was different—it was angry. The sea seemed to be in sympathy with him, in the same state of mind.

My mother told me that when he got back to Nablus he seemed to have aged ten years. For twenty years he had kept an image in his mind and when he went to find that image, it was no longer there; he felt like a stranger, excluded. It was a bitter, hard experience. When you have been forced to leave your land in such a tragic way the thought of returning never leaves you. There will always remain a nostalgia and the desire to turn the clock back. It was terrible to feel suddenly like a stranger, shut out, powerless. He told me about that journey with such sadness; it marked a most important date for him. For years he had looked forward to that moment and when it came it was more bitter than all the waiting. Something in him broke. He had to admit that a part of his very self had been cut off and torn apart.

My father decided one day to take me to the sea at Naharia, to show me that part of Palestine that I had only seen as a child. It was a very emotional journey and I will never forget it. We traveled in a small truck, which gave us a sense of adventure, sitting up high, surrounded by the countryside. My father knew every centimeter of that land and pointed out each plot: "That belongs to so-and-so."

But now these lands were the property of the state of Israel. He noted all the changes, the fields that were cultivated differently. The old map was stamped on his brain. He could show me the remains of the villages that had been destroyed and depopulated, and knew all their names. I gazed around and understood that everything had been wiped out. It was almost impossible to believe that a little more than twenty years earlier there had been villages in the places indicated by my father. I kept staring, wanting to fill my heart up with this land. I knew that the struggle had been very long.

In those twenty years we Palestinians had remained separated, isolated from one another, with almost no contact. Between the Palestinians of 1948 and those of 1967 there was a big gap, a profound distance. The Palestinians of 1948 who had remained in the state of Israel were ghettoized, oppressed, and treated very severely as a minority. They had led a closed life for twenty years. They felt like prisoners in their own homes: they no longer had the same vitality, nor even the same chance of resisting as those in Jordan and Gaza, who had been able to live through a period of great political and cultural development.

Suddenly, after 1967, there was intense contact between the Palestinians of 1948 and those of 1967. We hoped for a single secular state for all who were living in Palestine, and the right of return for the people who had been forced out, as had been proposed by the PLO in 1968. But this dream has still not been realized.

My father had changed in the years I was gone. I found him more fragile, but also more gentle. He wanted to spend time joking and chatting with me and the children. It was touching to see him leave the house proudly holding the hands of his grandchildren. I had never had a long conversation with my father and it seemed strange to see him like this. I wanted to hug him and make a fuss of him. But I couldn't—I wasn't used to it and I felt a little to blame for all the problems that my brothers and I had caused him. Those fights had actually helped both him and us mature. During the 1950s he used to scold us for our activism—he more or less hated the Ba'ath party—but at the same time he had been influenced by it. He was concerned for his family, but he thought about it on his own, and told my mother that we were right and that it really was not possible to keep quiet. These days he was on the ball, even politically.

My mother had also changed. She had rediscovered her talkativeness and her irony. She would discuss Marx and Lenin, and she would say that Muhammad was braver than Marx. She was in the habit of reading the newspaper in the morning to get the first news of the day. She kept a little radio on her lap so that she could hear the news. She listened to it twenty times a day. She knew all the world news. She would talk about Italy's problems with me and amused me when she would say: "But this Italy, how come it is like this?" She listened to political and social analyses, and took an interest in people's problems. She was better informed politically than many educated people. She regretted that there had been no schools for women in her day; if there had been, she would say, she would most certainly have become the Minster for Public Education, or a poet, or a writer. And she may have been right—she certainly had the strength, ability, intuition, imagination, irony, and language.

My parents' attitude to my sisters had also changed. I had never been allowed to go to the cinema, or go out whenever I wanted. I had had to get married at the traditionally prescribed age and it had been difficult to persuade them to let me attend university. But it had been different for my sisters: they had been able to go abroad without any of those problems, obstacles, or discussions. My rebellion had cleared the way and interrupted the plans. My leaving for Kuwait and Damascus proved that it was not the end of the world, nothing terrible had happened.

Society had also changed; more young women were finishing their studies and were concerned about things other than getting married at an early age. My parents were open to new ideas; they did not remain closed-minded and bound by tradition. They had managed to understand the breath of freedom that their not very obedient children had introduced into the house. Moreover being parents of so many children had somehow forced them to understand the times. Even parents can sometimes learn from their children. And they were proud of theirs.

My month's permission was soon up. During our last days, Ruba caught the flu and had a high fever. It was summer and very hot; it was difficult to think of such a long and uncomfortable journey with a sick baby. So I went to the military governor to request an extension until the child was well again. It was denied: they told me that if I wanted to stay, I had to pay a tax for every extra day I spent in Palestine. I was humiliated and hurt by this arrogant request. To stay in my own home with my parents I was supposed to give money to a stranger who was occupying my land and laying down the law by force.

Of course I refused. I left with my sick child. Buses jammed with people, long waits, checkpoints, hours on line in the sun; terrible exhaustion, a whole day spent in crossing a few kilometers. Above all, it was humiliating. The word "humiliating" is the one I repeat the most when I talk of this experience because it is truly the word that best explains how I felt.

Saudi Arabia

I returned to Italy and resumed my normal life, but with a calmer, more tranquil rhythm. My Italian was improving and I made some deeper friendships. The children were growing older and attended nursery school. Finally I managed to have some time for myself.

There were a lot of difficulties still. We continued to live off the money from Muhammad's family in Saudi Arabia. It humiliated me to be dependent on others when we were such a large family. My pride was wounded. Moreover, I was tired of always having to think about survival—I had other goals and plans and did not want to wait any longer. I wondered what kind of future we could have that would suit us. I had always had it in mind to move closer to my own country. I did not want to deprive my children of their family, relatives, and roots.

In 1975 we decided to take what was possibly a decisive step. I would go to Saudi Arabia to work, taking my children with me, and we would stay with my husband's family; he would remain in Italy to finish his studies. We had been thinking of Saudi Arabia as a country where we might want to live. We were not allowed to return to Palestine and we had no relatives anywhere else.

My three children and I left for Riyadh. It was terribly hot in Saudi Arabia, unbearable, the temperature above 100 degrees. But my husband's relatives welcomed us with great celebrations. They were a great, old-style patriarchal family. We all lived together in a huge house with a courtyard in the middle, surrounded by a veranda onto which all the rooms faced. We were assigned a space in the house and we began to settle in. It was fun to be among so many people taking care of us.

I began to look for work immediately. I gave a lecture at a private school and was offered a teaching position. My daughter, Ruba, was enrolled in the same school and attended first grade. Ra'ed went to nursery school and Sultan was enrolled in the third grade of elementary school.

Teaching and contact with colleagues made me very happy after such a long period of anxiety and frustration. I put my heart into teaching and tried to make real contact with my pupils. As in Kuwait, the teachers were young women from Egypt, Iraq, Syria, and Palestine, interested primarily in their salary at the end of the month. But I was not like that. I saw that the young girls often came to school listless and uncommunicative. They were Arab, but many of them had been born and lived in America or Europe. They had difficulty with the traditional way of teaching practiced in Saudi schools. I helped them open up and not let themselves be isolated.

The teaching curriculum was a big problem. Religion was pervasive in all subjects— everything was explained by the use of religious names, images, and ideas. It was enervating; there was no relief. So I tried—with a little flexibility and without going against the system—to introduce other arguments. I began by saying that a woman has her own dignity, that she should be equal to a man, that girls should learn to read, and that marriage should not be their only aim. I taught passionately and I made progress. The girls would go home and talk about their special teacher who told them to read and study differently. Fortunately their families, who were often well educated, were not scandalized by my methods and even appreciated them.

I had the chance to do other work, too. I did some translations for an Italian firm that needed someone who knew both Arabic and Italian. They paid well and offered good benefits, but I had to do the job secretly, because women in Saudi Arabia were not allowed to hold such positions.

I would get up early in the morning. My brother-in-law would take the children to school at an hour when it was still very cold and a bus brought them home at about three in the afternoon. After dinner and a short pause we would retire to our room and there I spent many hours helping the children with their homework. At the end of the day I was very tired from working two jobs.

My great tragedy was Sultan. He felt isolated at school. He could speak a little of the Palestinian dialect, but didn't know the Saudi dialect nor classical Arabic, which was taught at school. Nor did he know how to read, a little like the girls in my classes. In a way this was a scandal. I was a teacher of Arab literature and my children did not know Arabic. They even said I was "an Italian who teaches Arabic literature." Some of my pupils' parents protested.

Sultan was always very angry when he returned from school: he would say the he had been beaten and scolded because he couldn't sing. By singing he meant reciting the Qur'an, which is very difficult to do even for someone who has studied it. Imagine what it was like for someone who had never spoken the language. He was very good in mathematics and in English, but naturally in other subjects he was at the bottom of his class.

Sultan's school was exclusively male—women were not even allowed to enter—so I could not go and speak with the teachers in order to learn first-hand how things stood. So I sent my brother-in-law instead. The teachers told him that everything was fine, but Sultan continued to say that they ignored and bypassed him. He was an exuberant young boy, and was used to doing well, so this was a difficult psychological situation for him. It was easier for Ruba, because she was in first grade and attended the school where I was teaching. I knew her teacher and could ask her to give Ruba a little extra attention.

Ra'ed went to nursery school. He was in a class with a prince—an emir, the youngest child and only son of the minister of foreign affairs, brother to the king. The little emir had to be pleased in everything. Ra'ed was a beautiful blue-eyed child and always dressed a little differently from the others. Perhaps the little prince thought he was like a vision, since he wanted always to be with Ra'ed and share his toys and his snack. This prince had a slight skin infection that made him somewhat ugly. He was very tiny and dark-skinned, and there was absolutely no way that I could convince Ra'ed to accept his company. Nor did he believe that he was a prince: for him princes were like the ones in the fairy tales, handsome, charming, radiant.

The child's father came and threatened the head-master of the school: if Ra'ed would not make his son happy, he would have to take measures. The headmaster, trembling, came to ask me not to make difficulties and to persuade Ra'ed to play with him and accept his snacks. There was no arguing, the wishes of the snotty little kid were more important than anything else. So it was that one day I went to the nursery school and spent the morning break with them, holding their hands and trying to bring them together. Ra'ed never said a word, but simply put up with it. But that was not enough. Now the little prince wanted to invite Ra'ed to his house for a snack. It was not considered desirable to send one's son to the palace, and people did not look on it favorably. So I had to invent thousands of excuses to the little emir's Swiss governess to avoid those undesirable visits. It was absurd. Those people thought everything was at their disposal and woe betide anyone who did not go along with them.

At that time Saudi Arabia had an iron regime and considered itself the guardian of religion—at least as far as appearances went. It was not permitted to smoke in the street; men could not wear long hair; women had to be covered up; the *abbaya* was a requirement. There were no cinemas, no theaters, nowhere to spend an evening. If you did not adhere to the rules, you ran the risk of being expelled.

In this respect Kuwait was different—it had changed with the times: there were restaurants and bars in the hotels and many other meeting places. Compared with Saudi Arabia, Kuwait seemed like paradise.

I had daily clashes with this closed, backward male society in which there was no role for a woman. Men and women were isolated from each other. It was almost impossible to meet outside of the home—there were separate entrances in all the buildings and stores. Women made friendships with the women who lived in the same apartment building, went shopping with them, and passed all their time with them. Their role within the house was important, but outside they had no rights, no freedom, and no chance to intervene. For example, by law women were not allowed to work or to drive. It was supposed to be enough to be a wife, satisfy her husband, and make children.

The women in our family accepted this role as natural and had no difficulty obeying the rules—in fact, never questioned or discussed them. The woman was queen of the house, the duty assigned to her by God. They could not understand why I so desperately wanted to work. They told me in our discussions that I was selfish and that I was sacrificing my family by my behavior.

I have always been strongly aware and wanted to be a free woman. I could not accept their arguments. But I was most disturbed by the need to offer my children explanations.

The *abbaya* itself did not upset me, because as I have said, it really protects very well from wind, sun, and sand. But it was very difficult for my children to get used to seeing me covered up in that big black garment. They cried and kept telling me, "Don't put it on! Don't put it on!" I told them that I wore the *abbaya* to protect myself from the dust, and that it was the tradition, and I didn't want to create problems for their grandparents.

One day some laborers came to do some work in the courtyard and we women had to remain shut up in our rooms. Ruba wanted to go out and I tried to think up a good reason for the restriction. I told her we could not go into the courtyard as it would disturb the workmen and make them angry.

I refused to teach her that the culture forbade women from being in the presence of men, but, since she had to live there, I could not teach her to rebel against these things. So I tried to hide what I really thought; I would dramatize and find answers acceptable to a six-year old. I needed a lot of imagination to come up with all the explanations that were needed.

I realized, living there, that it was impossible to ignore the way of life. The burden of such an experience began to weigh on me and I gradually understood that we were strangers, just as we had been in Italy. In fact, my children were less strangers in Italy than in Riyadh. Ra'ed had actually been born in Italy. When we went out onto the street in Saudi Arabia the other children would shout in chorus, "Italians, Italians!" My children had had to overcome the problem of being different in Italy, and now they had to face the same thing in an Arab country.

Living in the midst of such a large family began to wear on me, too. We were not free; we had to turn to my sister-in-law for everything we needed. It would have been different had my husband been there, but I could not get impatient with my brother-in-law and had to wait passively and silently for certain favors. Everyone was very kind, but I had been used to acting on my own—at least in small matters—for years: I had come and gone as I wanted.

The children missed their father a great deal. I, too, missed Muhammad; I felt like a teenager in love. During school breaks, I would happily tell my colleagues about him as if we had just met. They would say to me: "You won't stay here long—you are too much in love with your husband." And that was the truth. It was painful for my husband, too, to be so far away from us.

I began to wonder what the sense was in continuing to live there. What did I want from life? The only argument for staying in Saudi Arabia, the only reason that would hold anyone in that desert, was money. As in Kuwait, people could not break away from it. They followed the God of Money, the God of Work. It was the only thing they talked about during evening conversations.

I soon realized that it was not worth the effort. I missed Muhammad, I missed Italy, I missed a freer, more civilized

177

society where a human being was valued. I wanted to teach my children to be strong, independent, and responsible, capable of making decisions. But in a society such as Saudi Arabia one could only suffer in silence, sacrificing one's own voice. The price for economic security was too high.

The Saudi Arabian experience lasted only six months.

We were so happy to return to Italy. The children never stopped singing "Long Live Italy!" They had felt oppressed and suffocated in Saudi Arabia; they had had to live through certain experiences and share customs that were not satisfying.

Ruba, for example, had been very upset by the killing of a lamb on the last day of Ramadan. It was a bloody event, and the Saudi children were used to it and took it in stride. It was a terrible experience for Ruba to see the tender, little white lamb with whom they had played, have its throat cut.

Still today my children have not been able to wipe out the memory of some of those experiences; they come to mind whenever we talk of Arab countries and especially Palestine. It is something that makes me very unhappy. I try to make them understand that it is not fair and that they should erase such ugly memories. Fortunately Ruba returned to Saudi Arabia on one occasion when she was grown up and enjoyed it. She found that people there were also kind and humane, and had the same problems as people anywhere.

Stability

The experience in Saudi Arabia marked a significant turning point in our lives, resulting in the decision to remain in Italy. Our children seemed to emerge from a nightmare. They were in seventh heaven when we arrived home. They were as delighted as if they had been released from prison.

Tears came to my eyes hearing them sing and yell "It's great to be home, it's great to be home!" There were parties to celebrate their return. Six months had gone by, the school year was not yet over, and their school friends had been waiting for them all that time. My children felt encouraged by such a warm welcome.

Ruba had to finish first grade and found the seat she had been assigned at the beginning of the year still empty and waiting for her. The teacher had told her classmates about her and they were curious to get to know her. With my help and that of her teacher she managed to make up what she had lost and was promoted with little difficulty. Ra'ed was in nursery school and so everything went smoothly. Sultan was very brave: it seemed that he had left school only for a few days and he fit right back into his class. They were happy: their return among friends seemed to restore their calm.

For my part, I emerged from this experience for what seemed the umpteenth time with much clearer ideas. I felt calm, tranquil, free of many problems. Until then I had placed a lot of importance on my husband's graduation. Now I understood that our lives could not be bound by this. I had a better understanding of what I wanted and was able to assign the right importance to what mattered. I was still very much in love with my husband, despite our great differences of character; I loved him and it had been hurtful to live so far away from him. At last I could look at life with calm and security.

Also, I no longer felt a stranger in Italy. I saw that I was more of a stranger in certain Arab countries like Kuwait or Saudi Arabia. I understood that my dignity as a woman, my freedom as a human being, the simple ability to come and go and make decisions, were essential to me. I could not do without them. Nor did I want my children to do without them. They were not worth giving up for a bank account in Saudi Arabia.

Europe had grown during the period that the Arab world looked on and fell under the dominion of the Ottoman Empire. It is true that in the past, Arab civilization had been more important than that of Europe, but now things were reversed. I was experiencing the contrast between these two worlds. In one was democracy, freedom, individual respect, and in the other, a grievous situation for women, with profound limits on individual freedom. In one, a person could even challenge the actions of the government; in the other, the same action might cost one's life.

Also, I wanted to put an end to the precariousness. I was tired of so many years on the move, always without a fixed home, without even the possibility of staying put. It was time to make an important and definitive decision. And so it was that we made the decision to live in Italy permanently, in the hope that, should the day come when Palestine would be liberated, we would be able to choose between our country of origin and our adopted country. This decision reassured me and enabled me to confront all the problems of our life.

In the first place, we should no longer depend economically on others—it was too humiliating. I had refused to do so when I was twenty—how could I do so at thirty-five? I told my husband that we had to find more secure employment for him and for me, something suitable to my abilities, so that we could depend entirely on ourselves. In no time I found employment as a translator in an import-export firm. I acted as interpreter at fairs and also became a fur salesperson. I managed to take care of my children and the house. My husband also found remunerative employment and began to travel frequently.

I felt at ease—I was calm and I was making friends. They were mostly Italian friendships. I knew some Palestinians living in Parma but they were very young, students enrolled at the university and I looked on them with kindness and affection, like brothers or children. I always liked to have a house full of people, to prepare Palestinian meals for them, and to tell them about Palestine.

What It Means to be Palestinian

I wanted my children never to forget that they were Palestinian, that they were born of Palestinian parents, and that they had a land and roots where their grandparents lived. I wanted them never to lose interest in anything that concerned Palestine; I wanted to bind them to their origin. I used to tell them the history of our land, of how it had been torn apart, of how the Palestinian people, who were so proud, strong, tenacious, and aggressive, had been tricked and massacred.

I wanted them to learn to value their difference, the non-Italian part of themselves. I realized that Palestine was slowly becoming a part of their life, of their school work, and of their games. I remember Ra'ed as a little boy wanting to play a game of Israelis and Palestinians rather than cowboys and Indians. Of course the other children did not understand: Israelis and Palestinians were strange words for them so they would go home and ask about them. When I met their parents they would ask me how a child so young could know all that. I explained that it was because of our home environment and our history. Ra'ed had written an essay in fifth grade on Ayatollah Khomeini and the teachers were astounded. My children also absorbed their culture from my sisters and brothers and my husband's relatives when they came to visit.

Our brothers had grown up by now. They had all gone to the university and had been involved in politics. Each made his own choice in respect to culture and politics, and each went his own way, so that they were scattered across four continents. We had always had a wonderful relationship, so I never felt alone.

The ties with my sisters grew with the years, especially with Nadia and Badia who had been very young when I left. Now our friendship had become strong, a deep bond, solid and lasting. We were like the three musketeers—"All for one and one for all." Perhaps it was the awareness of how important such a relationship was that had encouraged me to have a large family.

Through all these years, we siblings have continued to see each other at least once in a while. Italy is the ideal meeting place for anyone coming from Jordan, Lebanon, Tunisia, America, France, or Germany. It was important for us to get together, for the children to know each other and live together for a while.

We used to go camping in the summer in Lignano Sabbiadoro. I remember how bewildered a family once was by the sight of our children and the five different languages being spoken. They could not tell where we came from and took bets among themselves, but no one came near to solving the puzzle. Finally one of them came and asked for an explanation. We answered that we were

Palestinians, and we began telling them about Palestine, about our life far from home and far from each other, and about our children who were forced to live in so many different countries.

Contact with my brother Ihsan and with my parents, who were still living in Nablus, was much more difficult. I never saw my father again after my journey in 1972. Ten years later I returned to Palestine for his funeral.

Also my last visit to Palestine had been the occasion of a tragedy: the death of my sister-in-law, Ihsan's wife. It was in 1984. I was on holiday with my family at my sister's in Tunisia when the dreadful news arrived. I had an Italian passport and so was the only one of us who could leave immediately. It was a terrible tragedy that had shocked the whole of Nablus. Her death was absurd—she had left for Jordan to get the documents needed to enroll her two oldest children in a computer school and she had taken her youngest child, a baby girl of only a few months, with her. When she was on the Allenby Bridge she began to feel ill, overcome by exhaustion, the heat, and anxiety about the checkpoint. She used to suffer from asthma. When she arrived in Amman, she went to bed and died shortly thereafter with the children playing beside her.

The Israelis managed to make problems even on that occasion. The body was supposed to be sent home by the Red Cross, while the children had to return on their own. But the children were on their mother's passport and she was no longer there to accompany them. The Israelis used this as an excuse to try to prevent their return. I saw my mother again on that occasion—now she would have to take care of her grandchildren. I left wanting to stay near them and help.

I saw my mother a couple of times again after that journey, at Fiumicino airport, on her way to my sister's house in Tunisia. We met for a few hours and spent most of the time arguing with the customs for permission to talk to each other up close and not through a grill. Fleeting but intense meetings—the meetings of Palestinians.

Motherhood

The responsibility for educating our children fell to me. My husband was always at work. His return home in the evening was always a magic moment for the children. He would cuddle them and do anything they wanted. My role was the reverse: I was with them all the time and, rather than being concerned with their immediate wishes, I thought about their future.

I have tried to educate my children to be independent, to get along, to share their life with others, and to be serious about their studies. I saw to it that they learned to stand on their own two feet as I had had to do. I had had to rely on my own strength in order to get ahead, and I wanted them to acquire this ability also. I had learned how difficult it was to know or imagine the future, and that one always has to face it alone and with determination.

I tried to make them understand the importance of

their culture: I wanted them to read and be interested in so many different aspects of reality—school was not the only important thing. I tried to interest them in politics. They read newspapers and listened to the news from an early age. In our house watching the news was a ritual. We felt that it was very important that they become actively involved in politics. I have never agreed with people who watch and criticize from a distance—people should organize and become involved, rather than standing by twiddling their thumbs.

I was always very fond of my eldest son because to a certain degree he had been the victim of all our negative experiences. It is true that he received the usual attention given to a first child, but he also experienced the hardships of the war of 1967, the sacrifices of our life in Vienna, my sadness and disappointment. This was followed by life in Italy where he did not understand a word and felt different from the others. As the eldest son he was burdened with the responsibility for his younger siblings and our expectations as parents. When our plans became clearer and life more calm, I was able to help him. I told him about my experiences, about his family and his country, and other parts of the world. I talked about my favorite writers, the books I read, and my passion for Russian literature. Thus, when he was still a young boy, Sultan read Dostoevsky and almost all the Russian and English classics, philosophers such as Nietzsche and Sartre, poets like García Lorca, Baudelaire, and Ginsberg. We would discuss and exchange ideas and impressions. Many of these ideas gradually took hold in his mind. Unfortunately Sultan was not able to find the right friends who could appreciate his ability and stimulate his inner experience. As a result, these days he is often dissatisfied, melancholy, and perplexed, searching for something he cannot define.

I remember encouraging him to assert himself and stand out at school to compensate for the feeling of being different, of not being Italian. This he did for a while and then he realized that it was not worth the effort. He no longer felt the need to prove his worth to others. He simply wanted to be himself. This made me happy: I realized that he was thinking with his head and was able to make his own decisions.

With Ruba the experience was quite different. I wanted her to grow up with the conviction that it was a privilege to be a woman. Perhaps I overdid it; I am always too enthusiastic and don't know my limits. I used every opportunity to stress the need to struggle for one's rights, to resist the injustices suffered by women in Arab countries, in Italy and in the world. I am a feminist, but I have always thought that men were an important part of our life. I have always loved men but saw them for what they were, with all their limitations. Since my earliest years my eyes had been open and I had learned to see them in a rational way. I have never thought of them as exceptional beings. In fact I have always thought that women were superior to men.

I would tell Ruba what I thought. I wanted to save her from my own experience. I wanted her never to go to the back of the line, never to give way to everyone else, never to lose herself in another person, never to deny all her own needs in order to serve others. Ruba must learn to achieve her own space; she must experience the joy of feeling equal to or even better than men.

And so the pupil outdid the teacher! Ruba today is firm in her ideas, free and independent, and I often seem to her backward, narrow, and limited.

Maybe she is right. I am aware of being full of contradictions. I grew up in a society in which women were deprived of their freedom and, even though I rebelled against this culture and education, I know I have been influenced by it. I find myself the daughter of two cultures, with one foot in each. In theory, I understand all the rights my daughter claims, her wish to enjoy her sexuality and her emotions, and yet I cannot bring myself to allow her them. We often quarreled—I could not help interfering, but at the same time I understood that I did not have that right. I knew that she should be allowed to live her own life and grow from her own experiences.

Despite this we have had a calm and open relationship, the complicity of women.

Our third child, Ra'ed, was the perfect son, the son everyone wants. He was a sweet baby, beautiful with blue eyes and straight blond hair, a clear complexion, not much like us. Everyone calls him "the Italian," because he was born in Italy. Even we call him that to tease him. He has never felt different; he is the one, of all of them, who has been most influenced by Italian society. His childhood was very calm, with no great problems. He was always full of ideas, imagination, a big chatterbox, an absolutist, with a real predisposition to command.

Then he, too, reached a time of crisis, when he was in conflict with his parents, his siblings, and with the whole world. In order to attract attention and distinguish himself from the others, he would take the opposite position, he was always on the other side, in politics and in everything. Now that crisis is over and Ra'ed has matured, he knows what he wants and is determined and ambitious, open-minded and well informed on many problems. He is gifted with great learning ability and success comes easily.

My children are grown now. I have tried to share my values with them, and to instill in them security and trust. I have taught them to think for themselves, to resist injustice, and to choose freely.

I know that the future holds many uncertainties and I have learned at my own expense that life is full of difficulties; yet I believe I have succeeded in giving my children a foundation for facing life. In this, I am content.

About the Intifada

My ties with Palestine were never broken; my political interest in everything that concerned Palestine never waned. Certain connections can never be broken and one would have to change one's skin to alter them. But my involvement went through a very long period of lethargy.

After 1967 we often wept and raged at what was happening to Palestinians both within and outside of Palestine. First came Black September in Jordan in 1970, followed by the bombardment of the refugee camps, then the massacre at Tal al-Za'atar in Lebanon in 1976, the Israeli occupation of Lebanon and the massacre of Sabra and Shatila in 1982, as well as the pressure exerted on Palestinians by Syria. All this was tragic. The Palestinian people, at the mercy of other countries' interests and conflicts, have always had to pay for it all. Sometimes they were exploited; at other times they were driven on by so-called friends.

For years no one wanted to listen to the arguments of the Palestinians, and that is what eventually led to terrorism outside of Palestine. I always thought that this sort of terrorism should be condemned, that it was unjust and stupid. I hate violence and I have tried to communicate this to my children. I have explained to them that true strength lies in the strength of the word, in logic and justice. Even if, in reality, this isn't always true. But I do understand the reasoning behind those who carry out these acts. They think that the whole world is against them and is responsible for their problems and that they have nothing to lose.

I myself was disheartened after so many defeats. I had hoped and trusted in the future and in the Palestinian people, but everything appeared black to me. We never seemed any closer to a solution. Europeans think that there is a solution for everything, but those of us who have borne these tragedies cannot think that way.

It felt impossible to feel the enthusiasm and hope of my youthful battles. I was no longer ready for prolonged and serious political work. I felt old and had lost faith in my own abilities.

I would go to public demonstrations and debates and stand in a corner listening. I wept and shuddered as I remembered our times of struggle. It disturbed me to think of the freedom needed to establish one's own ideas and I thought about the suffering we Palestinians had to endure just to establish that we are a people. I would return home shaken, full of a huge nostalgia, and with a perplexed and troubled mind.

Following the invasion of Lebanon and the massacre of Sabra and Shatila in 1982, I felt a surge of energy when people in Italy began to talk more clearly about the Palestinian problem, about the Communist Party, about proletarian democracy. The mayors showed great solidarity and came to an agreement in support of Palestine.

At the end of 1987, the intifada broke out. The Palestinian question leaped on to the front page of newspapers. My daughter, Ruba, began to take an active role in political life. She was called on to represent Palestinians on public occasions. But it was a problem for her, because she had been born in Vienna and had grown up in Italy. She had an Italian education. Nevertheless, her sensibilities were Palestinian and she was nostalgic for Palestine and felt strongly about it. So naturally she began to rely on me and once more I found myself involved in political work.

My first involvement was a debate at Riva del Garda, on the occasion of the Festival of Woman. I was very moved. I was not sure I would be up to it, but everything went well. Basic things don't change. When you have learned to ride a bicycle, you never forget.

I have begun again to attend meetings, debates, party celebrations, and pacifist gatherings. I have rediscovered the richness of knowing so many people, especially women, new friends. I have rediscovered the world and the atmosphere that I loved.

This is a particularly favorable time: my sons are grown up and I have a marvelous husband who does not oppose me and, on the contrary, takes pains to be near me. I can be away from the house as much as I want and I can dedicate myself entirely to this activity. I feel successful and rejuvenated. I am extremely happy. For the first time after so many years I feel alive and useful. I can contribute to the Palestinian cause.

I have found again my faith in my own ability, and have acquired strength and confidence again almost out of the blue. It is a golden time, better than any since I left the Arab countries. During that time I confined myself to looking at the world through a window, to reading the newspaper, and chatting privately; now I have reentered the liveliness of public life.

My type of involvement is more political, focused on Palestine. I participate as a Palestinian woman, a Palestinian living in Italy, the daughter of my experience and my culture, absorbed into a country that is not my own and is not an Arab country. I am different from the Palestinians who used to live in the Palestine of 1948, and from those who have come to live in Italy only recently and are not able to open up and make real contact with Italian society. I am different from the Palestinians living in the Occupied Territories who have to deal with very concrete problems and risk their lives on a daily basis. I am different from the Palestinians living in refugee camps or in exile in Arab countries or in the rest of the world.

I bring with me my own individual experience of exile, which has taught me the importance of being united, of overcoming division in order to forge a common objective. Distance from the theater of events, preoccupation with sensitizing public opinion to our problem and obtaining results outside of Palestine, drive me to remain above specific discussions of the political choices of the various components of the PLO. Yet I have never thought that the heated debate within the PLO and among Palestinians was sterile. I have always seen in it an example of democracy as well as a natural and inevitable fact, especially among those who are struggling and risking their lives.

I tell the story of Palestine that has remained unknown and misunderstood for so long. I talk about the origins of the problem, dating from 1948, about the struggles the Palestinians have always had and I explain that the intifada that has so shocked Westerners cannot be separated from the earlier struggle of Palestine, from the daily efforts that the people have always made. Men, women, children, and old people—they are all opposed to Israel, have always protested, sabotaged, and attacked. It is natural to look at the Israeli jeeps with eyes on fire or hurl stones at them, but it is only now that this form of struggle has become so visible that the West has taken note of it. I don't want people to think that the Palestinian people have suddenly woken up. With the intifada, the daily struggle of people against the injustices and the violence of the soldiers and the Israeli settlers has simply become organized. People's enthusiasm and hopes have increased and their fear gone away. Out of the intifada, peaceful organizations have emerged in which women and children can participate. Women have had marvelous experiences within the feminist organizations. Once again I can feel proud of my people, who are capable of being renewed and of imparting a lesson in civilization, courage, and tenacity.

In Italy it is the women, most of all, who give concrete support, who join in solidarity with the intifada. I think there is more solidarity among the women because they do not have very official roles, and are not afraid of losing any benefits. They have the courage to make their opinions known with more clarity and strength.

My rediscovered political involvement gives me the opportunity of meeting the friends at the House of Women in Turin, the group known as "Visiting Difficult Places," an initiative which in its humanity and courage mirrors a typically feminine involvement. Also, I have friends from the Documentation Center of Women in Bologna, from the Association for Peace, and from many other groups.

These encounters involve me in initiatives that have at their core the problems of European Arab women, their rights, and their struggles. Even though I have expressed reservations about some of the initiatives of these groups of women, I am interested in participating and making a contribution. Encounters with Palestinian women bring to light great differences. For Western women, the goal is no longer equality with men, but rather the search for an identity, a space, a role in which to express their own difference, their capacity for an autonomous strength. For Arab women, who have not always been allowed to work outside the home, and who have not been granted the right to express a political choice by voting, their deepest aspiration is for equality of rights, for the ability to work side by side with men.

As a result of the activity of the women's committees born out of the intifada, Palestinian women now have a greater awareness and openness and are better able to understand Western women's experience of autonomy, even though for them the fundamental need is to maintain unity among Palestinians.

I look on my political activity with women as an important part of my life. Although I have shared with men many stages in my intellectual formation, I feel more at ease with women, and I find there is a greater opportunity for discussion and understanding. I think women have a different way of looking at life and politics. Motherhood teaches women to be practical. Our protective instinct makes us peace-loving, enemies of war, and sensitive to the great problems of humanity.

Many new friendships have been born in this active, lively atmosphere in Parma and throughout Italy. These are deep friendships that I was lacking in the past, and they have freed that part of me that I kept subdued for years. They fulfill my need for in-depth, constructive political exchange.

They join with the wonderful friendships of my early years, those born in the condominium and parks, through the schools and the children, formed of an intense complicity.

Once more I have found, as in the old times in Nablus and Kuwait, women friends with whom I can talk about clothes or children, or personal matters, and friends with whom I can organize debates and demonstrations. Different women, different stories, but a profound bond among us all.

And now my friends are helping me in this new struggle against an illness that limits my freedom and prevents me from living a normal life, slowly destroying my energy, my enthusiasm, and my joy in activity.

But it is difficult to speak of this new, grievous experience.

Epilogue

"Every Time, the Thrill of a New Beginning"
Memories of Salwa in Her Final Years

In the final pages of her memoir, Salwa gradually moves into the present; her story fades and becomes vaguer and more incomplete, providing a striking contrast to her quite clearly defined recollections of adolescence and the years in Kuwait and Vienna, or to the decisive narrative of episodes and people prior to her birth, such as those of her mother and father in the Palestine of the 1930s.

Such a contrast is probably typical of the processes of memory: well consolidated remnants emerge from more distant periods, having grown more precise over the years. They are once more inscribed into a life that is now complete in every way, so that events, moments, feelings, and thoughts can be recalled against a well articulated background—as though reinvented through her own reinterpretation of herself. Immediate experience is still unclear, influenced by developments that cannot yet be precisely identified and whose significance will be modeled on future outcomes.

Moreover, in Salwa's case, the "today" reached in her autobiography was a situation made dramatically precarious by her cancer. The entire examination of herself and her own existence could not help but be deeply marked. After all, Salwa herself was the one who chose to begin her account with her notes from the hospital in Houston, in which she immediately indicates clearly that she wanted to leave traces of herself in a book, "something palpable," while withdrawing from the complete and constant contact of her daily life, as well as from the historically important events in which she was immersed.

Yet, even in the unhappiness of certain moments when she found herself deprived of the possibility of new experiences, Salwa remained a person of extraordinary vitality, capable of showing passionate interest in all dimensions of experience. So here I would like to try to evoke at least a tiny spark of her efforts to participate and her readiness to form new bonds that marked her last years. As for the pain caused by knowing that her future had become vague, it is fitting for us to remember how many of us grew close to her, knew her, and became her friend.

"I am a Palestinian woman"

My use of "we" in these pages needs explaining. I, in fact, knew Salwa both at home and in a context shared with other women. Our efforts to explore various ways of dealing with conflicts led us to the experience, in 1987, to which Salwa herself alludes when she mentions the network "Visiting Difficult Places" with its various local formats. Its focus was to form relationships among both Israeli and Palestinian women that would allow them to share in the search for reciprocal knowledge and exchange, a path that led to many visits to Jerusalem as well as to many opportunities here in Italy for debate and encounters.

It was under these circumstances that several of us got to know Salwa, and the contact was all the more significant in that it demanded of us a very real effort to truly listen in order to understand and respect the differences. The deepest core of her identity—as she herself defined and perceived it—can be found in the very first sentence she dictated on tape when she began working on this book: "I am a Palestinian woman." To carry on a dialogue with us, there-fore, was far from easy: the effort of creating an autonomous perspective as women provided a solid base for a relation-ship, but our task of trying to take into account the events, needs, and expectations of both parties was certainly not immediately acceptable to someone who could only live as a Palestinian.

The relationship that developed was both profound and honest, but never accommodating. Salwa was passionate in her demand for authenticity in regard to herself, to her roots, and her own sense of belonging. At the same time she sought a true comparison, and was prepared to examine herself in the light of other journeys and other experiences—provided that it stimulated an honest discussion, without preconceived obstacles or avoidances. As I met her from time to time in meetings in Bologna, I gradually became aware of the different realities of the women involved in building relationships between Palestinians and Israelis. It became particularly clear when it fell to me to participate with her in some public debates.

A particular example came at the end of March 1990 when we were both invited to a meeting in Piacenza to discuss the passage "from difference to differences," which formed in those years the basis for an exchange of research among women. Some months earlier, the international initiative "1990: Time for Peace" had brought hundreds of people—mainly women—to Jerusalem from various parts of the world, and a short film was shown before the debate in Piacenza. We saw—or rather we saw again—so many exciting images: Women's Day and the protest that had welded—both physically and symbolically—a coming together of Israeli and Palestinian women in a single march across the two parts of Jerusalem; the human chain that embraced in a multinational circle the walls of the city. But we also saw the gap between the festive climate in the Jewish zone and the stationing of police and soldiers in the Arab zone. Or rather, against the background of these demonstrations for peace, what was happening in the Occupied Territories at the same time—the destroyed houses, struggling families, blockades, occupied settlements, violence, and intolerance—was a harsh contrast to the efforts at discussion among so many men and women who were working to bring about fundamental changes.

Salwa was the first to speak, giving voice to her emotion. She said that every time that she saw images like these she felt enormous rage at the tragedy of her people, torn from their roots and threatened with extermination in the name of the right of force. She then went on to trace a very detailed historical framework of the events that took place over more than a century—from the beginnings of the Zionist movement, Theodore Herzl, the Ottoman domination, the year 1917 and the Balfour Declaration, up to the present, by way of 1948 and 1967, the wars and the international political choices that had been made (the West's support of Israel, but also "the hypocrisy of the so-called Arab brothers who had used the Palestinian cause to obtain advantages for their own regimes"). What she wanted to emphasize was an awareness of how long the situation had existed—before the beginning of the intifada, despite the distorted vision the world had created. It was important to speak of the long journey during which their disappointment, rage, and uprooting were transformed into a refusal to live as refugees, into the desire to take destiny into their own hands, into the capacity for self-determination shared by millions of Palestinians scattered across the globe. Moreover she herself, as she indicated in the final pages of this book, resumed her public commitment during her final years and emphasized that her choice and her wish was to "to continue to tell the story of Palestine that had been so long ignored and misunderstood, by speaking of the origins of the problem."

As she punctiliously recalled dates and events, quoting official acts, numbers, statistics, Salwa relived her story with the strength and torment of her emotions and her experiences. And so, after I had taken my turn in seeking to present the plurality of the ties we were forming with Israeli and Palestinian women, she asked me a very bitter question, expressing the importance of her own personal experience as a key to existential reconsideration, rather than ideology, politics, and history. She asked, "But how do the Israelis feel when they see the refugee camps? Or the Russian Jewish families when they arrive and occupy the houses of others—do they not ask themselves who was living there before?" It was this that concerned her. She had been driven from Jaffa in 1948 and then, because she was living outside of the country in 1967, found herself finally exiled and unable to attempt any contact with Israeli women. The debate continued in the same spirit, because the two of us and many other participants were trying to avoid abstract assessments or cutting judgments of blame or justifications of right and wrong, in order rather to confront the subjective irreducibility of the experiences and the tension involved in creating real areas of respect for the diverse or even converging needs to exist, each within her own identity.

"I am not moderate; I don't know how to compromise"

Salwa describes herself as an "extremist." It is true that on the occasions I have just described and many other times later, I have always heard her present her convictions enthusiastically—but she also knew how to listen to other points of view and discuss them honestly. The intensity of any of these disputes did not lead to rigid conclusions. The Piacenza conference developed even deeper ties among us because we understood that the differences would not be resolved by ending the dialogue—rather, they demanded a renewed willingness to continue the debate.

That day in Piacenza, however, was the first time that Salwa talked to me about the severe pain she had been suffering for several weeks. She did not seem too preoccupied by it, but in fact it was the first sign of the illness that was taking over her existence. Yet she was still full of life and interests. After the debate we left together, she for Parma and I for Bologna, where I was to meet with a group of students who, as members of the Panther movement initiated in 1990, had pursued their discussions along these lines. We spoke about them at length because Salwa was linked to their world through her own children. She was particularly excited by the new feminist ideas that could come from young women like her daughter Ruba and her contemporaries.

Then came her first surgery in Italy, followed by recuperation in Houston at the end of the year. Salwa was forced to give more and more energy to what she herself called, in the last lines she wrote, her final "struggle." She drew on her exceptional resources of vitality to resist the devastating advance of the illness. Even more than from her tremendous capacity for physical resistance, these resources resulted from her own tenacious love of life, her daily pleasure in recapturing her life, as much as from her anxiousness to remain in contact with what was happening in the world. For months there were long telephone conversations or visits to her house during which discussions of her health, treatments, clinical evaluations were mixed with long and extremely lively debates of every new fact from the Gulf War to the end of the Soviet Union and to the negotiations with Israel, initiated in Madrid. Salwa's desire to maintain her grip on the world meant that she always found enough energy to be excited in her comments and exchanges of opinion, even with her failing voice and breath and in the midst of the most painful fits of coughing. All the while she remained the center and hub of her home life and she would tell us with amused irony how Muhammad or her children were doing. She wanted to retain control so that everything was done the way she wanted.

She was very clear about what was happening to her, and she wanted no pretense from her doctors. She knew that the various procedures would only delay, not block, the course of the malignancy. But she was determined to gain, one day at a time, as long and full a period of life as possible. From the beginning, she hoped for a year or two, measuring them against the life of her children, wanting to leave them more as adults, having finished their studies. Then, inevitably, the horizon became ever more restricted. Once she had started on her autobiography, the end goal was at least to finish her story, if not to see it materialize into a book. This too gave her a deep desire to live, a way of reacting and finding a perspective that would allow her to remain alive longer. From the first timid and fearful suggestions—But does it make sense? Who would be interested in my life? Isn't it an unjustified presumption?—the decision to take on the reconstruction of her own life and through it, to provide a glimpse of a part of Palestine, grew stronger every month. In the end Salwa became so attached to the project that she talked of it as "giving birth to a child," but the pain of more cruel moments made her realize that, nevertheless, she might not see it and the idea that the book would see the light of day only after her death made her feel like a ghost.

The last occasion that Salwa participated in a collective meeting was in Bologna at the end of November 1991, when we came together as part of the Visiting Difficult Places network in order to discuss a plan for a seminar with Palestinian and Israeli women. Salwa—in one of her typical "excesses"—told me that she wanted to participate, even if it "were the last day of her life." In fact, she did appear, but she looked so debilitated that we were all very upset and simply tried to make her understand somehow how much we all cared for her. She stayed only a short time, did not take part, but I think that being there gave her relief: despite everything she was still able to participate.

I saw her for the last time in the hospital at Parma at the end of February 1992. She was by then very ill; but that day she had a slight reprieve and I found her sitting up in bed reading the manifesto. So once again we spent several hours together, talking about her, her treatments, what the doctors said, but also about her children's exams, Muhammad's work in Berlin, and of the journeys he made in order to spend as much time with her as possible. Then we spoke of the book, how it was going, what point Laura had reached in her rewriting of the work, what she herself had been able to do, rereading some of it. It took a lot out of her, though. She also told me with great excitement of the meeting she had had at the beginning of the month with Marina Rossanda, who had sought her out for an interview for the magazine *Balsam*. She had been dismayed because she had felt weak and incapable of organizing her ideas, and was in tears as she waited for her. But then, once the interview started, she had felt fine; she had felt an immediate sense of friendship and it had gone very well. She had already received the transcribed text and wanted me to read it. We talked about it at length and later discussed it with Ruba, when she came by with a friend. Once again Salwa demonstrated for me her persistent curiosity about life, surrounded by her loved ones and her interests. We said goodbye in sadness but also serenity, knowing that it might be the last time we met.

"The joy of being active"

Many friends, both men and women, came to Salwa's funeral a few days later. They were from many different backgrounds because, through her great ability to communicate on various levels, she had built many different but always authentic relationships. So many men and women had known her as a person full of strength that the grief at her departure was profound. But almost to emphasize that the nucleus of her life was rooted in the history of Palestine, her family's grief was also the grief of the diaspora: only three sisters and one of her brothers were able to come from the various parts of the world in which they lived. Her mother was in Tunisia and there was not enough time for her to get a visa and be able to leave from Nablus, once she knew that Salwa's condition had deteriorated. News of her death reached her en route and at that point the children, out of concern for her age and health, thought it best to stop her.

Leaving the cemetery we found ourselves again in the little group of those who had become Salwa's friends through our political relationships as women, and who now had gathered from Piacenza, Rome, Modena, Padua, Bologna, Turin, and Naples. We began to share ideas on how to honor Salwa's wish to remain present in some way: should we adopt a Palestinian child from abroad? Or manage a nursery in Nablus? Or consider a scholarship to enable a young woman to come here and gain the maturity and autonomy that were so important to Salwa? In any case, we all agreed that the part of her that must not, at all costs, be forgotten was her passionate involvement, that "joy in being active," which remained constant through to the last pages of this book.

Forty days after her death, according to Palestinian tradition, the family organized a memorial for Salwa in Parma. It was a moving and evocative evening and, as many different people remarked, it was also "strange"—that is, beyond our normal customs and very far from any kind of ritual rhetoric. The voices of men and women alternated in speaking of Salwa as they had known her, some in earlier times, others on the more recent occasions of her return to public involvement. In particular, two of her friends from our network—Luisa Morgantini and Giovanna Calciati—recalled the beginnings of what was to become a relationship of many with her. The first connection came through her daughter; Ruba had participated in a demonstration as a result of the intifada, presenting a remarkable portrait of a Palestinian student with the Emilian accent of a young woman who had grown up in Italy. It was Ruba who had wanted to get her mother involved. For those of us from Turin, the name of Salwa for many months was synonymous with "that great Palestinian from Parma."

Laura mentions in the Afterword her first meeting with Salwa, when we went together in March 1991 to her house in Parma. I, too, remember it very vividly, because I sensed in both of them the emotion as well as a certain fear at embarking on such a demanding undertaking. Would they between them have the empathy necessary to work well together? Would they be able to establish such a profound ability to communicate with each other for the one to find in the other an interviewer who could review her life and create a successful narrative? The anxiety quickly evaporated as soon as Salwa greeted us with her characteristic warm immediacy, and began to describe the way she envisioned organizing the account. She immediately conveyed its fascination through the liveliness with which she evoked situations and feelings and through the amazing richness of the events and the people we could begin to imagine.

Thus began a complex relationship and from her first enthusiasm for the project's interest, Laura was able to offer extensive availability as well as great tenacity. To immerse herself within a life story demanded a very great emotional involvement and not only an intellectual but also a constant psychological involvement, all the more so because of Salwa's deteriorating condition. It was certainly not a smooth process. Gradually, as the story took shape, the obstacles multiplied. There were Salwa's own problems, the exhaustion of making sense of her own life, her own affections, her ties with her origin, and with those constructed over time. She was constantly torn between her spontaneous inclination not to accept compromises and, on the other hand, her sincere preoccupation in not being unjust toward others and respecting the feelings and events that lay beyond the images left in her memory.

But it was also difficult for her to put trust in other ways of speaking of herself. This resulted in frequent differences of evaluation, constant discussions as to which were the best choices, as much from the perspective of style as in the selection of themes, the unresolved weave of agreements and contrasts. Stemming from the anxiety about the short amount of time at their disposal, there were moments in which the urgency of remaining present throughout this story of her life almost exasperated her as she made the effort to retain control of a process that she knew would escape her. In many ways, the effort of launching this book into the world was Salwa's final expression of that tormented "desire for freedom" that had characterized her since adolescence: her need for autonomy and at the same time her awareness of the limitations, a continual tension between her impulse to listen only to herself and her own "excessive" desires, and the lucid realism which time and again persuaded her to be very firm in her decisions.

"Desire for freedom"

As Salwa had feared, she died before the work was finished and each of us—Laura, Giovanna, and I, at our various levels of involvement with her in the commitment to its completion—was left with an even heavier responsibility in many ways, because greater strength was needed now to make choices that were faithful to her. The relationship with Ruba became crucial: not as a formal guarantee of respect for her mother's wishes, but for her ability to pick up and resume the story. Ruba, in fact, managed immediately to find the courage to become immersed in rereading the text, checking names and dates, seeking suitable images, and embarking on discussions of the decisions that had to be made. At the same time, she was able to recover her own life and her own interests and projects, after almost two years of complete absorption in caring for and being close to Salwa.

It seems almost banal to acknowledge that Ruba has much of her mother's energy and desire for activity, nor does it do justice to the intense interweaving of continuity and diversity that is at the root of the ever more happy relationship of daughter to mother. In my very limited experience from my visits to the house, it seemed to me that Salwa knew how to form ties with all her children of true friendship, frequent discussions, and a real openness of confrontation. This was especially so with Ruba, because of Salwa's earlier passion for a young woman's open spaces.

It gives me pleasure to end with an acknowledgment of some of the many threads that continue today to extend the relationship with past years. Above all there is this book that Laura has successfully brought into existence; thanks to her work and her strength in bringing conciseness to the narrative, I think that those who read it will experience precisely what Salwa wanted: those who knew her will recognize her salient features, but also those who meet her through this story for the first time will be able to sense her strong presence that leaves its mark on our memory.

And then there is the account of all the happenings that form a part of Salwa's life and her presentation of herself as "a Palestinian woman." Last August I was in Jerusalem with Ruba and Giovanna (a project that Salwa had longed for for her daughter, when I told her of my journeys to Palestine and Israel and she would ask me whether it might be possible to go with Ruba). I felt great nostalgia visiting the house in Nablus, getting to know Salwa's mother, and feeling how accurate her descriptions had been when she described her as proud and solid "as a rock." But I also experienced much joy in seeing how Ruba not only sought traces of her past, but made passionate efforts to build her own relationship with that world, as it is now and as it therefore is changing. Her decision to write her Ph.D. thesis on the Palestinian women's movement, by researching the reality and the expectations, the weight of traditions and the tensions surrounding innovative projects on the rights of women, seems to me a truly fine way to delve into a story while at the same time questioning it and finding her own autonomous perspective.

The spirit of Salwa's testimony provides a pause in which to measure the possibility for change. She said each time that she faced a new day or a new phase it was marked by "the emotion of a beginning" and "the desire for freedom." The path to this freedom may rest precisely in the ability to keep a grip on reality, to understand the processes beyond the illusions and disappointments, yet at the same time to act, as Salwa did, with all the strength of one's own experience and the urgency of one's own desires.

—Elisabetta Donini

Afterword

Salwa the rebellious, the curious, the adventurous, Salwa who did not want to die, who wanted to remain among the others. Salwa with the wind in her hair. She was born in 1940 in Palestine, where she spent her adolescence. She lived for many years in Arab countries and spent her last twenty years in Italy.

I met her for the first time on March 27, 1991, at her home in Parma. We had been introduced by Elisabetta Donini, a member of a group from the Turin House of Women called Visiting Difficult Places and dedicated to forming ties between Palestinian and Israeli women. I was finishing my studies at the university where my field of concentration was oral history and anthropology; I was also involved in the Middle East and had recently visited Palestine with Elisabetta. Salwa was looking for someone to whom she could dictate her life story. She had often thought about it casually; with the outbreak of the intifada she had resumed her political activity, particularly among Italian women, and she began to give it serious consideration. She was encouraged in this by the curiosity and insistence of her new friends, especially Giovanna Calciati, who had spoken of it to Elisabetta. The serious illness that had struck Salwa about a year before we met gave her the impetus to turn her dream into a reality. I was to assemble her story, which in turn would become the primary source for my thesis in cultural anthropology.

I remember the great smile that lit up her slightly oriental eyes and her curly, constantly moving black hair. She always looked and listened attentively; nothing escaped her, not the slightest sound, not a word, not a gesture. Sometimes she would assume a serious rather than worried look, a firm voice, and peremptory tone. She would sit cross-legged on the couch in the style of her countrywomen. Her house was simple, basic, as Arab houses often are.

She had already begun to plan her story and was able to identify the most important facets, which she communicated to Elisabetta and to me. From her very first comments, surprising segments of her life emerged: the lively atmosphere of the 1950s in Nablus, the many men and women who were the models for Salwa's identity, the relationship among Arab countries, especially the contrast between the Jordanian regime and Kuwaiti society, and the relationship with Europe. Her family history is also the history of a segment of Palestine from the 1930s to the present day.

We worked together for a year on this book. I often went to Parma, and stayed for two or three days at a time. The Palestinian house where she lived with her husband and three children, all a little younger than me, was generously opened and I was made to feel one of the family. Given the difference in our age, my relationship with Salwa followed a bit of a mother-daughter pattern: she expressed herself confidently, and I was deeply aware of her authority. I tended to identify more with her children, my contemporaries. I formed a deep friendship with Ruba.

During that year, Salwa's illness progressed relentlessly. In the last months, my visits to her were almost exclusively in the hospital. By the summer of 1991, we had recorded 25 hours of tape. Salwa had narrated her entire life, starting from infancy, according to the plan she had drawn up. My questions were basically for clarification. Salwa reread the entire transcript, roughly four hundred typed pages, making changes and corrections. The end of the summer was followed by a period of in-depth examination, prompted largely by my questions as I searched for images and details to use and a clearer understanding of her experiences and the significance of her story. This resulted in the first written draft in which the material was organized chronologically according to the details of the story. Salwa reread this first draft as far as the end of the section on Kuwait.

Salwa died on March 5, 1992. I could still feel her presence around me and hear the echo of her voice from the written pages. Now I had to manage without her: a huge and terrifying responsibility. A second draft was needed to transform the text into a fluent and organic whole. My involvement of necessity became greater. Ruba's trust, her courageous and passionate participation at every step of the way, and Elisabetta's encouragement provided essential support.

I emphasized the thematic organization in order to maintain a significant chronology for the events and places in Salwa's life; some chronological details were modified. I integrated and reworked her thoughts based on what I had learned. I enriched some of the settings and images from my own knowledge and experience of the world described by Salwa. Some portions were completed from later information.

Salwa's desire to transform her life into a "novel" may be the key to understanding her personality and the psychological, human, and political importance for her of the story and the book. It was clear that she was creating a precise and complete image of herself. Faced with approaching death, of which she was clearly aware, she wanted to endow her existence with a wholeness and integrity such as belonged to the novels that she so loved, rather than to life. The hours she dedicated to the narration were some of the most important in her last year: Salwa found unanticipated energy; she became passionately involved, forgetting fatigue and illness. As she narrated, Salwa rebelled against death in the way she had always done when faced with events that might destroy her—with all the dignity available to a human being. Narrating and thinking about the book became the focus of her realization of herself as a woman, as an autonomous individual, of someone living in reality. Clearly she had chosen to spend the last days of her life in leaving traces and maintaining her ties with this world that had always stirred her curiosity. These ties and her consistently active presence are reflected precisely in the act of narrating. In fact, telling her story also meant that she was willing to create confusion and make waves. Salwa herself censored some things so as not to break with emotional and cultural ties, but others she made explicit in order to provoke thought, to make an appeal to the world. I am thinking, for example, of her criticisms of Arab men who were Marxists, as well as her constant emphasis on the West's neglect of the Palestinian cause.

These psychological and political aspects, the literary allusions and references to reality, are evident in her prologue dedicated to death and memory. A few months before we met, Salwa had been operated on in a hospital in Houston. It was there that she tried to overcome her loneliness by thinking back over her life and deciding to narrate it. In the first lines of the prologue Salwa, while still in a hospital room in Houston, sets the scene for her memories and her reflections on life. They were "dictated" to me toward the end of our work and were intended for the beginning of the book. The lines that immediately follow belong to a cassette that Salwa recorded one night, during her hospital recovery, when she could not sleep for the pain and the thoughts of death. They were words meant for me, not for the book, yet it seemed to me appropriate to include them in the text. Salwa was asking for a very profound commitment from me, and she was confirming the huge significance that the book had for her. She intended it to be a challenge and a vital link with the world.

The years of her adolescence in Nablus are those which she relived with the deepest nostalgia as she recounted them: years of dreams and hopes in the face of a life that was often harmed by events and circumstances. Her rebellious character, her excesses, adventures and memorable episodes, joy and cunning, emerge brilliantly in her narration of that period. Traces of them are scattered throughout her images and expressions.

The years in Kuwait are told with great calm. They represent for Salwa a period in which she gained economic independence and saw the growth of more mature desires, such as personal fulfillment, work, and family.

The difficulties of her emigration to Europe, her marriage and the war of 1967 brought about a break in her life; there followed years of defeat and disillusion, but years that also included profoundly important choices for the Salwa I knew: a complex woman, the sum of all her experiences and identities.

In her last years, Salwa resumed her political activity and returned to the old enthusiasms that had caused her the least suffering. I believe it was essential for Salwa to feel she was still involved in them but she could not speak of them at the time because her illness precluded any ongoing responsibility. At the same time, she dreaded speaking of them in the past tense, as it would imply that she had no future. This is why, at the end of the story, Elisabetta has written a few pages in which she records Salwa during those years of activity and initiatives on behalf of Palestine.

Salwa's exceptional qualities, the intensity with which she lived and her many varied experiences constitute the boundaries of her story but also provide its richness. Her story is of great interest partly because she was a fascinating, vibrant woman, but also as a primary source of knowledge of Palestinian society and history.

By refuting the stereotype that confines Arab women to a thick, heavy blanket of passivity, Salwa creates her identity as a woman, forged through confrontation with many different models, and achieves autonomy out of an extremely interesting masculine sphere. The number of feminine models with which Salwa compares herself is surprising. Remarkable also is the strength and independence of these Arab women. The grandmother, intent on organizing the marriage of her son. The mother, "this soldier, this horse, this rock," who was of peasant stock and proud of it, who once gave birth without help from anyone, who turns her prayers into a dialogue with God, and who was always knowledgeable about the principal questions of international politics. One of

Salwa's sisters, on the day of her funeral, told me that Salwa, of them all, was the one who most resembled her mother, with the same stubborn and tenacious character. On the other hand, her relationship with her mother was not so easy; Salwa often criticized her. She could not always identify with her and sought new models.

It was in fact a man, Adnan, her older brother, who became her window on the world. It was he who introduced her to the classics of Western literature, and it was he who sent her an airplane ticket to Kuwait and provided her with the chance to experience an independent life, to work and enroll in the university.

As she read the many books circulating through the house, Salwa encountered a new female model, one that was extremely different from that offered by tradition: Simone de Beauvoir. Salwa loved her and her books passionately. A rereading of *Memoirs of a Dutiful Daughter* reveals many of the elements that seem to have become a part of Salwa and her self-presentation: her fervid intellectual curiosity, her fascination with well-educated men, the desire for freedom and achievement.

Those same Arab women, the friends that Salwa speaks of, are women who are often inspired to find a new lifestyle: they are involved in politics, attend university, become teachers, and study and work in other Arab countries, in Europe, and in the United States. Their attitude to money, to themselves, and to their life is different from that of more traditional Arab women.

Even the sexual segregation apparent in Salwa's story seems to have different degrees and significance according to the historic and geographic context. But it is not enough. If we compare Salwa's story with the anthropological literature on Arab women, it seems that it is precisely this segregation of the sexes that is the origin, in Arab-Islamic society, of a strong, independent psychology of the women in respect to the male sphere.

In the more traditional segments of society, this psychological autonomy is revealed in the formation of strong networks among women. In Salwa, influenced by models taken from her beloved Western classics and from her own experience of emigration, the psychological autonomy takes on new elements. The men who appear in her narration, even though she often refers to them as models because of their initiative and their freedom of movement, are subjected to profound and often harsh critical scrutiny, which sometimes results in silence concerning the masculine universe that surrounded her. It is a fact that it was at the urging of other women that Salwa decided to tell her story, and she told it to a woman. In short, Salwa seems to have found her way to fulfillment precisely through learning to think independently like a man, an ability she acquired in her youth, then lost and finally regained even more powerfully through her contacts with Italian feminists. Psychological independence was a cultural resource that came to her aid in the sort of situation when political activity, study, and work were not enough to make her continue to pursue her aspirations and prevent her from limiting her own horizon to her family.

Similarly another cultural resource came to Salwa's aid in moments of difficulty: although she subjected the institution of matrimony to severe criticism (despite her initial idealization of it), motherhood and the education of her children were sources of strength and enthusiasm for Salwa. On the birth of her last son, she exclaimed "I thank you God for this splendid gift. And so, out of a lack of sexual knowledge and naivety I have made a family... If I had planned it, the right moment might never have arrived..."—a little slap at the Western obsession with controlling and planning one's life. Thus a reworking of traditional models, rather than their rejection, helped Salwa even in a non-Arab environment.

To follow Salwa in the network of relationships developed in the course of her life implies also some understanding of ethnic identity, especially of Palestinians. We come to recognize the way Palestinians think of themselves with respect to other Arabs and the West, leaving Israelis in the background. The latter appear in the early years of Salwa's life and then, after 1967, in a rapid and grievous encounter. Very many Palestinians who, like Salwa, were no longer able to return to the territories occupied by Israel in 1948 shared this experience.

Palestinians of the diaspora had contact with other regimes, other social settings, and with people with different identities from Palestinians, even though they were part of the Arab world. Salwa talks in particular of the difficult relationship with the Jordanian government, and of the contrasts with Kuwaiti and Saudi society; she even includes comparisons with Egyptians, Syrians, and Lebanese, identifying the specific Palestinian quality that she recognizes in herself.

Through Salwa's story we are also able to follow the lives of another segment of Palestinian society: that of the people living in the territories occupied by Israel in 1967. It is they who are participating in the intifada. Elements of the identity of this group of Palestinians can be seen in Salwa's description of her visit to her home in Nablus in 1972. Think, for example, of the experience on the Allenby Bridge, the images of Israeli soldiers, the arrests, trials and prison.

Salwa's story also reveals the fissures of social class within Palestinian society. Her own class standing is very evident from her cultural references and her network of relations. She always identified with the intellectual middle class wherever she found herself: Palestine, Jordan, Kuwait, Syria, Lebanon, France, Austria, and Italy. She only alludes to the people in the refugee camps, the workers in Kuwait, the waiters in Vienna; they remain background figures. Recognizing this is important for understanding the limits of the social and cultural environment she describes.

It is interesting to consider her class standing in relation to her experience of the West, of Europe in particular, a mythical place for the adolescent Salwa—the very "mother of civilization." She was able to dispense with racism at the German language school in Vienna by showing wedding pictures of her elegant dress and social milieu. Salwa does not discuss racism in relation to Italy, but she felt welcomed there precisely to the degree in which she found her appropriate social level with the Italian intellectual middle class.

It could be said that through her relationship with Europe—both her reading and her experience of emigration—Salwa added new elements to her identity. This mix of diverse identities becomes obvious even in her narrative style. She bears in mind both her Arab and her Western readers: the Palestinian story is addressed particularly to her Western readers, to earn their respect and sympathy. From this public, especially from the women among them, she seeks solidarity for her discourse on women, which she fears instead might cause upset in her world of origin. In fact Salwa is very restrained when thinking about the Arab environment; nevertheless she does not refrain from certain criticisms she considers indispensable, precisely because she wants to bring about change.

Her complex identity, both Arab and Western, is apparent also in her attitude to death: Salwa wanted to break the silence and solitude to which health care in Western society was relegating her: it must not be forgotten that her real desire to tell the story of her life was born in the aseptic wards of a Houston hospital. It was there that Salwa reconnected with the world by regaining the ability to narrate handed down to her through her mother and grandmother. On the other hand, an oral account was not sufficient—she wanted a book, a written document.

Salwa's story allows us to follow the development of certain aspects of the Palestinian problem from the 1930s to the present day. Aware of the West's attachment to an Israeli version of the events, Salwa wanted to bring to light a series of less obvious arguments. Like all revisions, even Salwa's version has symbolic and mythological aspects, so I think it is important to highlight the points that connect with factual reality. I will review briefly four crucial points Salwa touched on with particular emphasis.

The first concerns the origins of the Palestinian problem and the fact that Palestine had been struggling for its independence since the first decades of the twentieth century. Already in the 1930s, Jewish immigration was perceived as an ever more serious threat by the entire Palestinian population. Resistance to this situation found expression either on a diplomatic level, through the traditional leadership's confrontation with the English (who from 1922 on controlled Palestine under the Mandate), or through spontaneous struggles on the part of the people. These two levels found their unifying moment in the revolt of 1936–1939.

The second point relates to the events of 1947–1948, Israel's so-called "war of independence," which for Salwa, as for other Palestinians, represents the starting point of a series of personal tragedies. Because of the now well-known sense of guilt on the part of Europeans when confronted with the monstrosities suffered by the Jews in World War II, the birth of Israel is often buried in a positive myth. In reality, it came about in a bloody fashion and through the expulsion of Palestinians from their land.

Two elements in particular that have often been wrapped in powerful mystification emerge from Salwa's discussion. They involve the two phases of the war of 1948, which are somewhat confused in Salwa's account, since she lived through the experience as a child: The first is that of Palestinians and Zionists, which ends with the formation of the State of Israel (30 November 1947–15 May 1948) and the other is the Arab–Israeli (from 15 May 1948 to the end of the year). The first phase saw the beginning of the Palestinian exodus from their land. As we see in Salwa's testimony, the exodus most certainly was not the result of a spontaneous wish on the part of Palestinians, nor, as she goes on to say, were they following the orders of their leaders. Instead, it should be said that the principal cities and many Palestinian villages became the scene of violent fighting and that the Israeli armed forces often had recourse to various techniques, including terrorism, with the precise aim of terrorizing the Palestinian population and convincing them to flee. The most famous case—though not the only one—was the massacre of the inhabitants of Deir Yassin. The second phase was marked by the direct intervention of the Arab countries. Here, it is important to clarify that various sources, including Israeli sources, contend that the Israeli state had armed forces that were superior to those of the entire Arab states. Neither then nor on successive occasions was the Israeli victory that of a little David fighting the giant Goliath.

The third point on which Salwa was most insistent, and which is not always accepted, is the relationship between Palestinians and the other Arab regimes. Generally the Arabs tend to be considered as a single, threatening entity rather than as citizens of different cultures, belonging to states that in general are weak and backward, with divergent interests. Salwa provides the impetus to consider clearly two aspects of the relationship between Palestinians and other Arabs: the tormented adherence of Palestinians to Arab nationalism during the 1950s and 1960s and the relationships between the Palestinians of the diaspora and the Arab countries that accepted them.

The 1950s constituted a crucial phase in the history of the Arab world: a nationalist leadership emerged that was both secular and modernizing and strongly influenced by Marxism and interested in Arab unity. During those same years in Palestine, following the demise of the traditional leadership, a new leadership emerged, tied to the burgeoning middle class. One segment adhered to the pan-Arab dream, which was considered the only tool capable of liberating Palestine from Zionism. These were years of hope and enthusiasm. Indeed, Salwa paints a glowing picture of the emergence of a new leadership in Jordan. In this period Salwa was excited by the intellectual liveliness, the political meetings, the close ties with the West and its cultural products, the hunger for books. There seemed to be no divisions between Christians and Muslims, at least within Salwa's social class. (Her father, a practicing Muslim, did not hesitate to send his sons to Christian schools.)

The entire pan-Arab dream disappeared with the defeat of Nasser in 1967. On the eve of the 1967 war Nasser held a threatening stance against Israel, aimed not at attacking that state, but at shoring up his own, increasingly shaky leadership of the pan-Arab movement. Nasser was aware of his military weakness, especially since in the preceding years the Egyptian armed forces had been exhausted by a war with Yemen in the north. Israel did not hesitate to take advantage of the situation, and in June 1967 neutralized the Egyptian armed forces and their allies.

It also becomes clear from Salwa's account that 1967 constituted a break in the relationship between Palestinians and the other Arab countries: from that moment the Palestinians decided to use their own forces to engage in the struggle, which led to even further friction with the other Arab countries. The refugees of 1947–1948 and 1967 who found shelter in the surrounding Arab countries were often treated with hostility in various forms, for various reasons. Salwa's discussion is primarily of Jordan and Kuwait. The Palestinians soon became the majority population in Jordan and the government tried to nullify their specific identity through a politics of assimilation. In Kuwait, the governing authorities treated the Palestinian intellectual elite well initially, and their abilities were used to construct the country. Later, however, the growing influence of the Palestinians led to the outbreak of tension among the people, as again documented in Salwa's account.

The fourth and last point relates to the consequences of the Israeli occupation of the West Bank, Gaza, and East Jerusalem following the Six-Day War. The situation in the Occupied Territories was terrible from the first moment. Contrary to the international conventions for the treatment of populations in occupied territories in time of war, the system of military domination caused upheaval in the existence of an entire population. Expulsions, denial of permission to return to Palestine, arbitrary arrests, restrictions of freedom, summary processing, imprisonment with inhuman treatment, destruction of houses, seizure of ever larger portions of land, became from then on part of the daily life of every Palestinian. Moreover, since the end of the 1970s, civilian settlements have been added to the military installations in the Occupied Territories, again in contravention of international law. With the beginning of the intifada, these repressive political procedures became even more severe.

In September 1993, precisely when the editorial work on Salwa's text was coming to an end, an agreement was reached between the Israeli government and the PLO. Still, the destiny of Palestinians bore the burden of many uncertainties. To imagine the future, it is essential to understand what happened, and this was part of the political significance Salwa herself wanted to impart in her story.

—Laura Maritano